LET IT MARINATE

Antonwaun K. M. Johnson

Kingdom Winds
Publishing

FOREWORD

In the culinary industry, marinating meat prior to preparation versus after preparation is up for debate. Some believe that the process prior to preparation makes the meat more tender and adds flavor, while others feel that afterward allows the meat to remain soft and receive the marinade better. Regardless of before or after, the process of marinating is vital, as it allows the flavors to soak in and make an impactful difference.

The process of marinating over the Word of God is similar. When we take the time to read God's Word and allow it to marinate in our hearts and minds, it makes us more tender and adds to our lives. Joshua 1:8b () says that if we meditate on the Word day and night (in other words "Let it Marinate" in our hearts) and do what it says, we will be prosperous and have good success.

Over the years, I have been blessed with the opportunity to converse with Rev. Johnson, and he's always left me with something to marinate on. He has the uncanny ability to look into the meat of the Word and the situational side dishes of life to create a flavorful seasoning packet full of wisdom and encouragement, which has made an impactful difference in my life and the lives of others.

In these pages, you will find prepared seasonings for the many situations you may encounter in life. I dare you to open up these seasonings, sprinkle them on your heart, and let them marinate in your life daily. Allow them to soak in and watch what God prepares.

-Rev. Angela Robinson

DEDICATION

I am very proud to dedicate this book to the life and legacy of my grandmother Louise Johnson who was my rock, my supporter, my prayer warrior, my rose, my everything and to my heart that lives outside of my body, my son, Caiden Christopher.

I would further like to extend my gratitude to my family, my close friends, my spiritual father Bishop Gregory Fuller who unknowingly planted the seed for this book, the Macedonia Church of Augusta family, my ADP Augusta work family and Facebook friends as they have all contributed to my life as well as encouraged me to share the revelations given to me through the Holy Spirit. I would also like to thank Michael Merles Augusta Photography for my photo on the back cover as well as his amazing and abundantly blessed gift of photography.

Finally, I would like to thank you, the reader, for taking the time to read the words given to me by the Holy Spirit. I pray the words bless you as much as they blessed me. May God continue to bless you exceedingly abundantly above all you may ask or think according to His power that works in and through you!

PRAYER OF EXPECTATION

Philippians 4:6-7

During a morning commute, the Holy Spirit spoke one word that resonated in my spirit. The word was "expectation!" What are you expecting? Are you expecting? I don't know about you, but I am expecting some things from God! I'm expecting God to bless me any day now! I'm expecting God to exceed my expectations for His glory! I am not just expecting for me but expecting for those who believe and made their expectations known to God!

Matthew 18:19-20 says, "'Again I say to you that if two of you agree on earth concerning anything that they ask, it will be done for them by My Father in heaven. For where two or three are gathered together in My name, I am there in the midst of them.'" If I expect for you unselfishly, then I believe God will exceedingly and abundantly bless me with my expectation. We serve a God who is able to do exceedingly abundantly above all we can ask or think according to the power that works in us! I believe it; do you believe it? God has a miracle with my name on it! I am expecting it and receive it by faith. God has a miracle with your name on it! I hope you are expecting it and receive it by faith. I pray that God hears, receives, and moves upon this prayer of expectation!

Please join me in prayer:

"Oh, Heavenly Father, we come before You at this time, first to say thank You! Thank You for allowing us to see the light of day! Thank You for the breath of life! Before we move forward, forgive us of our sins. Forgive us of anything that we may have said, thought, or done that was not like You. Now, Heavenly Father, we come to You with our hearts filled with expectation! We enter into this moment with anticipation because all things are possible in You!

"Your Word reminds us that if we believe we will receive whatever things we ask when we pray, we will have them. If someone is expecting healing, may it be received! If someone is expecting a financial blessing, may it be received! If someone is expecting a new job, may it be received!

If someone is expecting restoration, may it be received! If someone is expecting transformation, may it be received! If someone is expecting deliverance, may it be received! If someone is expecting breakthrough, may it be received! Whatever someone is expecting according to Your will, may it be received! If they don't believe, then, Father, I ask You to receive my intercession on their behalf; let them see You and believe.

"Father God, we have a hunger and thirst for You. We will continue to chase after You. We expect an encounter with You and a move in our lives like we have never seen before! As we wait, we will praise You! As we wait, we will worship You! As we wait, we will give You the glory, for we know that our expectations will be received any day now! Lord, we seal this prayer of expectation in the name of Jesus Christ and consider it done! Amen!"

Related Reading

Mark 11:22-24; Ephesians 3:20

YOUR PRAYER WILL BE ANSWERED

Daniel 10:10-14

One morning, it was hard to get into the position that I assume every morning to meditate on the Word and receive a word. Instead of getting frustrated, I just relaxed and started my morning activities (at work). I could feel the struggle in my spirit but refused to be defeated by the struggle. As I was talking to a friend, another friend walked up and asked, "Where is the word?" My response was, "It is coming." When I returned to my desk, another friend asked, "Where is the word for the day?" Upon the second question about the word, the Holy Spirit led me to the account of Daniel and how the angel was being withheld from Daniel by the prince of the kingdom of Persia. My prayer to receive a word this morning was heard and answered.

How many times have you prayed and felt that your prayers were falling on deaf ears? How many times have you prayed but didn't see any results of your prayer? How many times have you been discouraged about your situation because it seemed as if God was not listening to your prayer? Are you praying in confidence?

1 John 5:14-15 says, "Now this is the confidence that we have in Him, that if we ask anything according to His will, He hears us. And if we know that He hears us, whatever we ask, we know that we have the petitions that we have asked of Him." I would contend that Daniel prayed with confidence and his prayer was heard. Daniel did not know his prayer was heard because the response was being held up by a spiritual struggle.

You are so important that the Kingdom of Light and the kingdom of darkness are fighting over you! You are so important that Satan will send out his soldiers to stop an angel from delivering your word or blessing! You are *so* important that God will dispatch help to the angel so His word can get to you! And when your word comes, it is *always* on time!

Keep praying! Don't stop praying! Stay focused and be encouraged! Don't be timid with your prayer but pray with confidence! As you wait on the Lord, keep praying! Do not allow yourself to think that, because you don't see change, your prayer has not been heard! Remember, our timing is not God's timing. A delay is not a denial. When God answers your prayer, it *will* be on time! Though you may be having a "night" moment right now, know that weeping may endure for that night, but joy *will* come in the morning! Keep holding on! Your prayer will be answered!

GOD IS

Exodus 3:14

Do you know who God is? In times of trouble, do you know who God is? When you are feeling down, do you know who God is? When you are experiencing good days, do you know who God is? You may be thinking, "Why am I being asked if I know who God is?" Sometimes, we forget who God is when things arise, but knowing who God is in our situation can help us in our situation (let that marinate).

God is Jehovah Jireh, our Provider!

God is Jehovah Rapha, our Healer!

God is Jehovah Nissi, our Banner of Encouragement!

God is Jehovah Shalom, our Peace!

God is Jehovah Rohi, our Shepherd!

God is El Shaddai, our Almighty God!

God is El Elyon, our Most High God!

God is El Mauzi, our Strength!

God is the King of kings and Lord of lords!

God is our Joy in the time of sorrow!

God is our Protection!

God is our Light in dark places!

God is our All in All!

These are just a few things that describe who God is to us. God is who we need Him to be when we need Him! Simply put, God is!

Related Reading

Deuteronomy 28:58b; Psalm 148:13

START OFF RIGHT

If your car is out of gas, you will go to the gas station and get some gas. If there is no electricity in a room due to a blown fuse, you will replace the fuse to restore the electricity in the room. If you get tired from a good workout, you will drink water to replenish your energy. We do the things necessary to restore physical energy but forget about our spiritual energy.

There is power in prayer! Prayer can heal! Prayer can energize you! Prayer can change things! Start your day off with prayer and start off the right way. Stop and pray in the middle of the day to help you get through. And before you lie down at night, close out your day in prayer. You will be amazed by the power of prayer. Don't delay; start today!

Please join me in prayer:

"Father God, this is the day that You have made, so we will rejoice and be glad in it. Thank You for allowing us to awake from slumber and see another day. As we prepare for our day, we ask that You decrease us and increase You. Increase You so the ministry in us may go forth and be a blessing to others. Increase You so whatever the enemy is planning, he will think again when he sees You in us. Increase You so we can deal with the obstacles of the workplace, obstacles of school, and obstacles of anything that may attempt to trip us up.

"We ask that You be with those right now who are battling strong, troubling winds. Be with those who are hurting and comfort them. Be with the sick and heal them. Be with the weak and strengthen them. Bring broken families back together. Fill the loss of a loved one with Your glory, Your presence. Change us so everything around us may change. Renew our minds, renew our hearts so we can truly be new creatures in Your loving Son Christ Jesus. This is our humble prayer, and it is in Your Son Jesus's name that we pray. Amen!"

STAY CHARGED UP

As I looked at my cell phone, I thought about how I constantly keep it connected to a power source due to the amount of battery it uses. Even when the battery is fully charged, sometimes I leave it connected to the power source so I can use a function that may require extra energy.

My brothers and sisters, we are similar to our everyday cell phone. For some of us, our power is drained during the week, and we seek a recharge on Sunday. For others, our power is drained during the week, and we seek a recharge on Wednesday (Bible study) and Sunday. The Word reminds us in Matthew 4:4 (NIV), "Jesus answered, *'It is written: "Man does not live on bread alone, but on every word that comes from the mouth of God."'*"

Your power comes from *the* power of His Word. His power works through those who allow the power to work within them (Ephesians 3:20 - "Now to Him who is able to do exceedingly abundantly above all that we ask or think, according to the power that works in us"). Stay connected to the Word so you can be fully charged every day.

NOT IN MY HOUSE

Joshua 24:15

If you were to enter through the front door of my house, you would be greeted with the words "As for me and my house, we will serve the Lord" on the wall in the foyer. The message is to serve notice to those who enter that they are entering a house whose occupants serve the Lord. You can serve whoever or whatever you desire, but when you come to my house, you will know that we serve the Lord. The message is also present to let ungodly spirits know who rests, rules, and abides in our house and that they are not welcome there.

Generally, when we hear the word "house," we think about a physical house which is a building that serves as living quarters for one or a few families (according to Merriam-Webster). Our house is our dwelling place. Our dwelling place should be a place of peace, tranquility, joy and love among other things. Yet we frequently open the door and allow negative things (or people) enter our house and disrupt the atmosphere (let that marinate).

For most of us, we spend a majority of our time Monday through Friday in the workplace. The workplace, in essence, is our second physical house. Though it is a place of business, it can also be a place of peace, tranquility, joy and love. But we struggle in our work house because we allow or accept things that are not of God to reside there. Maybe we struggle because we walk into our work house and leave God at the door (let that marinate). Maybe we struggle because we try to suppress the Light in us instead of letting our Light shine bright (let that marinate, too). Whether it is our home, work place, school, wherever, we should serve notice to the enemy that we will not tolerate any of his mess in our house!

It doesn't stop there. Our bodies are a house, too. 1 Corinthians 6:19 says, "Or do you not know that your body is the temple of the Holy Spirit who is in you, whom you have from God, and you are not your own?" It is important that we watch what we consume physically and spiritually. Junk food is not healthy for our physical bodies just like drama is not healthy for our spirits (let that marinate).

Not everyone can lay hands on you because you don't know what kind of spirits in them may try to enter your house. To really keep it real, you can't lie with just anything or anybody because you don't know the spirits that are residing in their house. Lying down opens your house to those spirits (let that marinate for a while).

The enemy comes to steal, kill, and destroy. Let's be honest. We have allowed the enemy to enter our houses and steal our joy! We have allowed the enemy to enter our houses and kill our happiness! We have allowed the enemy to enter our houses and destroy our peace. But thank God for Jesus who came so that we may have life and have it more abundantly! It's time to evict the enemy from our houses! It's time to kick anything (or anyone) that is not of God out of our houses! It's time to let the enemy know who runs *this* house! It's time to let the enemy know that checkout time is here! It's time to change the locks by changing our ways so the enemy will stay out after he has been put out! It's time to tell the enemy to rise up and rise out of your house! It is time to declare to the enemy that whatever he tries to do, it won't happen! Not in *my* house!

FEAR AIN'T IN THIS HOUSE

2 Timothy 1:7

It is amazing to see the development and growth of a baby. We get super excited when the baby takes his or her first steps. If you watch closely, the baby displays determination, perseverance, and most importantly, faith. At some point, the baby becomes uncomfortable in his/her position and begins to move out of that position. He or she begins to pull up to get out of the sit-down position. Once the baby realizes it can stand, it takes a step. Now, the baby may fall after the first step, but the mere idea that he or she took a step in the first place encourages another attempt. The baby will get up and try again until one step turns into many steps, moving it from the uncomfortable position of sitting to the more comfortable position of standing, walking, and, in some cases, running.

The world is huge through the eyes of a baby, yet babies do not let what they see stop them from growing. They step out on faith, literally. They have no fear, as they are not discouraged by the fall but encouraged to keep pushing. As adults, we can learn a lot through our babies. Many of us are in uncomfortable positions but lack the faith to move. We stay in the box because we fear what may be waiting outside the box. We don't go through the door in fear of what may be standing behind it. And because we are afraid to move, we blame others for *our* unwillingness to trust God to order and guide our footsteps.

If a baby has faith to move, you can, too! You *have* faith—Fear ain't in this house! Yes, you may take a step and fall, but you can get back up again! Yes, you may walk into the unknown, but God will show you the way. Yes, you may be comfortable in your current position, but what God has for you is much better than your present stance! God did not ordain us to have a spirit of fear, so it is time to let fear go! Your growth and development depend on you letting go of the fear to move. Tell that ungodly spirit that you have faith—Fear Ain't In This House!

Related Reading

Psalm 27:1; Hebrews 11:1

DON'T TAKE IT OFF

Ephesians 6:10-18

Plain and simple: we should keep the armor of God on at all times! Don't take it off! I've heard a few stories of our service men and women engaged in battle going days in the same uniform. In the midst of a war zone, the last thing you would probably be thinking about is changing your clothes, especially when bullets are flying all around you. If you are secured behind a shield, chances are you will not expose yourself or make yourself vulnerable to the enemy but remain behind the very thing that is protecting you. I don't think you would remove your helmet in the midst of a battle, as it could very well protect you from some type of head injury. As a matter of fact, football players will immediately put their helmets back on if they come off during a play. In the current era, you will never see a player execute a series of downs without a helmet.

Let's be honest. Very often, we may put on the armor of God but take it off just as quickly. We take it off when everything is going well in life, not realizing that we are exposing ourselves to the enemy like a turtle without a shell (let that marinate). We put on the armor of God for worship service on Sunday but take it off when the benediction is given. Sometimes, we put on the armor of God before leaving the house in the morning but take it off before we enter our place of work, school, etc. If we are going to take anything off, take off the negative helmet (i.e. negative thinking) that you put on before you leave your house. Take off the bad attitude! Take off defeat! Take off the things that contradict your faith! Take off your nasty ways!

Clothe yourself with love, understanding, peace, compassion, kindness, humility, patience, righteousness, and all of those things that are of God! And when you put on the armor of God, by no means take it off!!

FOCUS ON THE PROMISE

Matthew 14:25-32

How many times have you been in the middle of a storm and felt like you were sinking? How many times have you been in the middle of a storm and allowed your worldly sight to overrule your spiritual judgment? How many times have you been in the middle of a storm and allowed what was going on to hinder your focus? How many times have you been in the middle of a storm and things did not always turn out how they appeared to be?

The interpretations of the Scripture above are countless and vary based upon what you may be going through at the moment you read the Word and receive insight from the Holy Spirit about the Word. Allow me the opportunity to share what was given to me: "Focus on the Promise!" Let's be completely honest and transparent. Far too often, we focus more on the problems in our storms than the Promise standing with us in the storm! Why should you focus on the Promise? You should focus on the Promise because:

•The Promise is with you always.

•Trouble doesn't last always!

•Weeping may endure for a night, but joy comes in the morning. That joy is Jesus, the Promise!

•The spirit of fear will come upon you and influence you to be afraid. Remember 2 Timothy 1:7, "For God has not given us a spirit of fear, but of power and of love and of a sound mind."

When Peter stepped out of the boat, he was doing just fine because he was focused on the Promise! When he took his eyes off the Promise, he began to sink! But in an instant, Peter thought quickly and called out to the Promise! The Promise saved him! What is taking you so long to call out to the Promise? How far will you sink before you call on the Promise to save you? I love this account of Peter walking on water because it reminds us that, even when our "water" (problems, situations, circumstances, etc.) may get over our heads, it will *always* be underneath the feet of Jesus!

"Well, that sounds good, but you don't know the storm I'm in right now. As a matter of fact, why is God allowing me to go through this storm?" You are right! I don't know nor have a clue about the storm you are enduring at this present time. What I can do is encourage you to focus on the Promise during the storm! The Promise is the light that will guide you out of the storm.

"Why go through the storm and endure troubled times?" God provided safe passage for Moses and the children of Israel by parting the Red Sea. After they crossed over, the sea came together and conquered the Egyptians! After God's children made it safely to the other side, the waters came together to destroy the Egyptians! What I am trying to say is God will lead you through troubled waters because your problems or enemies won't be able to swim after you (let that marinate)!

Don't lose your focus in the storm. You can make it! You *will* make it! Your storm is temporary! As a matter of fact, we declare today that your storm is over now! Focus on the Promise, and the Promise *will* bring you out!

Related Reading

Exodus 14:10, 26-29

STAND STRONG IN THE STORM

1 Corinthians 15:58

Definitions:

Steadfast – firmly fixed in place; unwavering or determined in purpose, loyalty, etc.

Immovable – not able to be moved

As I listened to the sound of wind and rain during the early hours one morning, I was reminded that, while some small bushes or trees may break under the pressure of the storm, there is usually one tree that stands strong before, during, and after a storm. For years as a child, I watched the pine trees in my grandmother's backyard sway back and forth during storms. Though some limbs would fall, the trees themselves would bend but never break (let that marinate). These trees were steadfast and immovable by definition.

Like a tree, we should be steadfast and immovable during our storms. How can we achieve this? We should deeply root ourselves in God's Word. On the surface, we may appear small, but our spiritual roots should be big and run deeply in the fertile soil of His word. As soon as the trouble winds blow, we should not break but bend and stand upright afterward. Oh, we will lose some "limbs" (family, friends, stress, depression, burdens, etc.) during the storm. The main thing is that you don't break and fall when the "limbs" break off and fall (let that marinate, too).

How can you be steadfast and immovable during a storm? Prayer, studying, fasting, meditation, praise, worship, etc. Don't wait until the storm arrives to do these things, but do them at *all* times. When the roots of a tree are constantly fed, they will grow continuously and abound in the soil. When our spiritual roots are constantly fed, they will grow continuously and abound in the Lord. So, when we endure a storm, we may bend but not break! We will stand strong; we will be steadfast and immovable!

YOU SHALL LIVE

Psalm 118:17

My brothers and sisters, I want you to declare by faith today that you shall live and not die! Today is the day that you speak life over yourself! Today is the day that you speak life into your situation! Today is the day that you speak life even in the middle of your storm! You shall live and not die! You have been hurting for quite some time, and it is time to heal!

Today, surrender your pain, your heart, your burdens and place them in the hand of the Father, for His Word says in 1 Peter 5:7, "Casting all your care upon Him, for He cares for you." Release the hurt and live! Release the pain and live! Release the shame and live! I know you may feel like giving up and throwing in the towel. You are not alone!

I am not afraid to say that I've wanted to throw in the towel and give up! I am not afraid to say that I have wanted to throw up my hands and walk away! But each time I reach that point, the Holy Spirit reminds me who I serve! The Holy Spirit reminds me that this battle is not mine but the Lord's! The Holy Spirit reminds me that I was built for this, made for this, anointed for this, so I have to stay in this (let that marinate)!! The past storms did not take me out, so why should I give up, thinking that this storm will take me out? Let me remind you that He has brought you out of many storms. The storms did not take you out! You may be a little bruised and have scars from the storms, but you lived through the storms! You will *continue* to live!

Beloved, declare today you will live! I know you feel like giving up. Don't give up and keep the faith! You are in this season for a reason! Submission to your storm is *not* an option! Living is your *only* option! See, I believe in the Resurrection, so I know I will live! I believe in Jesus who is the Resurrection and the Life!! Do you believe this? We got this! If you don't believe it, then I will believe it for you and me! "We shall live and not die! We shall live and not die! We shall live and not die!"

You *shall* and *will* live!

Related Reading

John 14:25

CHANGE BEGINS WITH ME

Ezekiel 36:26

As I was meditating and seeking a word (if you thirst after Him, you will seek Him for a word), I heard the word "change." While listening to a song during my meditation, I heard the word "change" again. The Holy Spirit began to speak and said, "What are you willing to sacrifice for change, and are you willing to surrender for change?"

Oftentimes, we ask God to change our situations, change the people around us, but we miss out on one very key and important fact. God can change our situations or change the people around us; however, if *we* don't change, things will remain the same because *we* are the common denominator in the fractured areas of our lives (let that marinate). If *we* don't change but continue to do the same thing, then we can expect to see no change in our lives.

We want to change the "flat tires" on the cars of others but don't change our own "flat tire" and then wonder why we are not moving (really let that marinate). If your trash has a strong odor and you move it from the kitchen to the laundry room, the odor will still exist because it is still in the house. But once you change the location of the trash from the laundry room to outside, the odor will eventually go away, and the atmosphere of the house will be fresh.

Mahatma Gandhi once said, "Be the change that you wish to see in the world." Our problem is we want to change the world around us but not ourselves. Romans 12:2 says, "And do not be conformed to this world, but be transformed by the renewing of your mind, that you may prove what *is* that good and acceptable and perfect will of God." In order for change to happen in us, we have to renew our minds, renew our hearts, and renew our spirits. Your heart, mind, and spirit have to agree to change. If they don't agree, then change won't happen. Remember, our biggest enemy is our "inner-me." Transformation should occur in us first and be the example for the world to follow.

All of us desire some level of change to occur in our lives. Just like the atmosphere has to be conducive or favorable for rain to fall, the atmosphere in *you* has to be conducive or favorable for change to occur in you. I am convinced that when you speak change into the atmosphere, the angels take that word into the heavens, and then the heavens conspire change to occur in you as well as around you. I will boldly say from my *own* experience that if *you* change, things and people around you will change as a result of the change in you. When you change, things or people around you have no choice but to adapt to that change (let that marinate)!

If you desire change, surrender your ways for new ways. Tell yourself, "The change I want to see must first begin with me," and say it with conviction! When you change, your world will change! Change begins with you!!

Please join me in prayer:

"Lord, right now, we ask that You purge us, cleanse us, purify us, and restore and transform our spirits, our minds, our hearts. Pour any and everything that is not like You out of us! Fill us up with Your glory! Fill us up with Your Spirit! Fill us up with Your power! Fill us up with more of You! Fill us up! Let what You pour into us change us! Let the change we desire to see begin with us! Whatever is not of You, we ask You right now to remove it from us so we can change and be who You desire us to be. We are confessing our ungodly ways so You can have Your way in our lives. Do it for us, Lord! Renew us, restore us, change us, and let the change in us inspire others to seek You and be transformed! This is our prayer, and we consider it done in the name of Jesus. Amen!"

Related Reading

Deuteronomy 31:6; Psalm 51:10; Jeremiah 32:40

CHANGE YOUR GRASSHOPPER MENTALITY

Numbers 13:31-33

Oftentimes, we encounter or approach issues, obstacles, storms, circumstances with fear, apprehension, uncertainty, or any other action contradictory to our faith. In our minds, the battle is lost because of what our worldly eyes see: deception. We can quickly convert a mole hill into a mountain. We give our problems far too much credit than they deserve. The credit that we give them fuels their control over us (a car cannot run if the gas tank is empty...let that marinate). We allow what we see to determine our actions and outcomes of the situations, making the problem a "giant" over us.

A grasshopper mentality will convince you that you should seek God to pay a bill and cause you to fail to realize that the same bill will be due next month when, instead, God can give you the provisions to eliminate the bill (let that marinate). A grasshopper mentality will convince you to settle on someone who has the appearance of a husband or wife when he or she is actually a temporary project meant to *prepare* you for your husband or wife. A grasshopper mentality will convince you that you can't do no more than what you are doing now. A grasshopper mentality will convince you that you will always be the tail and not the head, always on the bottom and never on top!

It is time to kill the grasshopper mentality and take on the spirit of a conqueror! You are bigger than your problems! You are bigger than your circumstances! You are bigger because you serve a God who is larger than life, the biggest of them all, the One who cannot be defeated! If you walk with a defeated mind, you will be defeated. If you bow down to your problems, you will always be a slave to them! Change your thinking to change your situation!

David faced Goliath with his faith in God. It was his *faith* that supplied the strength and power of the stone that brought Goliath down and killed the giant. When you are faced with a "giant," don't make it more than what it is but bring it down with your faith. Matthew 17:20 says, "So Jesus said to them, 'Because of your unbelief; for assuredly, I say to you, if you have faith as a mustard seed, you will say to this mountain, "Move from here to there," and it will move; and nothing will be impossible for you.'"

Don't be intimidated by your situation, your circumstance, your storm but intimidate your situation, your circumstance, your storm by speaking about your God—the King of kings and the Lord of lords!! Change your grasshopper mentality!

CHANGE YOUR ORDER

Matthew 6:33

This thought is straight forward with no chaser, no extra additives, no fluff; it's plain and simple. The verse in Matthew tells us the order which we should follow to receive our blessings. Let's be honest; many of us have been operating out of order or are *still* operating out of order. We are missing out on blessings because we are not seeking the Provider of blessings. We are seeking the blessings and missing the presence of God! We are chasing material things and sleeping on God! We are seeking the gifts and not the Giver!

If you seek after God first, then the destiny God has for you will come! If you seek after God first, then the blessings God has for you will come! Your praise and worship should not come after a blessing is received but should come even when you haven't received a blessing. Your praise and worship should be about God and not the stuff He provides (let that marinate)!

When you seek God first, everything will fall into place. When you focus on your vertical relationship with God, He will take care of you and provide for your horizontal needs! Your life may not be in disorder if you would get in order and put God in His rightful place, first in your life! God is not an *option* but a *priority!* When God gave His only begotten Son to die for our salvation, which was a sacrifice *many* of us would not do, He put us first! Since He put us first, He should *always* be first in our lives!

Change your order and watch things change in your life!

CHANGED BY THE WORD

Jonah 3:1-10

As I was watching a little girl tell the story of Jonah in her own words, she mentioned that Jonah was upset and felt like a fool that God did not destroy the city as He stated. The little girl said that God told Jonah, "Will you never learn, My love? My love is great. It is greater than My anger, and it is for all My creatures. Didn't I give you another chance?" The eloquent words spoken by the little girl led me to go back to the Scripture and inspired this thought: "Changed by the Word."

If you are familiar with the account of Jonah, God specifically commanded him to go to Nineveh and speak to the people. Instead of Jonah doing what he was told, he did what he wanted to do (let that marinate). I don't know why we think we can hide from our omnipresent God. Jonah thought he was smart by boarding the ship to get away from God. He endangered innocent lives by not listening and trying to run from God (really let that marinate—stop running)!

Even when you think you are running, God has a way to let you know that your efforts are in vain. Jonah was placed in a position that left him with no choice *but* to surrender and submit to God. God will put you in a position, leaving you no choice *but* to surrender and submit to Him. When Jonah surrendered his ways, God sent him on his way to do what He commanded him to do: preach to the people of Nineveh. Here is where the thought comes in.

Jonah told the people of Nineveh that the city would be destroyed in forty days. God was not pleased with the city, and His anger arose against the city, which is what led to the message that it would be destroyed. I would contend, based on the Scripture, that the people believed the word Jonah delivered without hesitation. We know this to be true as verse 10 lets us know that God saw their works. He saw them turn from their wicked ways, so He showed them grace and mercy by not destroying the city. The people of Nineveh were changed by the Word!

The Word of God should be transforming! The Word of God should change things in our lives! The storms you endure at work can be changed by the Word! The challenges you face with your family and friends can be changed by the Word! The storms you endure with "self" can be changed by the Word! The strain in your relationships can be changed by the Word! Oh, to be changed by the Word, you must hear the Word, and to hear the Word you must have a relationship with the Word (let that marinate)!

We serve a God of second chances! If God gave the people of Nineveh a second chance after they received His word, then He will do the same for you, too! He is the same God then, now, and forevermore. When God gives you a word, receive it and embrace it so you can be changed by the Word!

YOU ARE THE LIGHT OF THE WORLD

Matthew 5:14-16

Jesus said that we are the light of the world, and whether you know it or not, others are looking at you! It really became obvious to me that others are watching me when they shared what they saw in me as I endured (using past tense, believing my storm is over) my storm! I was blessed to hear others see God working in me and feel Him encouraging them to keep pushing.

Transparency has and will continue to be part of my ministry. Transparency is the condition of being transparent or allowing light to pass through so that objects behind can be distinctly seen. My transparency allows God's light to shine through me for others to see! I like to think that His light shines upon us and also reflects off us for others to see! Why do you think the room changes when you walk in? Why do you think people who may be experiencing a dark moment smile when you enter their presence? Why do you think people look forward to being in your presence? It is definitely not you nor me but Jesus in us that others see!

If you turn off a light, the light can't be seen. If you hide a light, the light can't be seen. If you allow your storm to hide *the* Light, others can't see the Light guiding you through your storm! If you allow your circumstances to turn you away from the Light, others can't see the Light turning your circumstances around!

We are the Light of the world, and we should let our Light be seen by the world. Don't be ashamed of the Light that shines in you and through you! Don't dim the Light burning bright in you! Let your Light be seen by others! For some people, you may be the only Jesus they see! If they are looking for Jesus, let them find Him in you! If others are drawn to the Light in you, introduce them to Jesus who resides in you! You may be the only peace they see, so let them find peace in you! You may be the only joy they see, so let them find joy in you!

Whatever someone is seeking, allow them to see Jesus in you and find what they need! Remember, you were once lost, and it took the Light shining bright in someone to guide you in the right direction. It is your turn to be the Lighthouse for others! We are the Lighthouse that could lead a lost soul to Jesus. We are the Lighthouse that will help a lost soul find its way! We are the Lighthouse that will give someone hope and lead him to the ultimate Light!

When you let the Light shine, the Light will bless you and bless those who are watching you! Don't hide the Light! Let it shine, let it shine, let it shine! You *are* the Light of the world!

CAST YOUR OWN STONE

John 8:7

When Jesus was approached by the scribes and Pharisees with a woman who was caught in the act of committing adultery, they wanted to see what He had to say about the matter. Under the old law, the woman was supposed to be stoned. Instead of Jesus being a judge, He performed an action that placed the responsibility of the woman's outcome back on the ones who sought Him for direction. He did not deny the law but simply challenged them by saying, "He who is without sin among you, let him throw a stone at her first." This statement convicted them, and they left, leaving the woman unharmed. Of course, Jesus did not condemn the woman, as He forgave her for her sin and commanded that she sin no more.

In our day and time, we know there are a lot of people who will still cast a stone at you. There are some people who have sinned in secret but are quick to call out the visible sins of others. Unfortunately, there are some people who will put others in hell for their sins but will justify their sins still worthy enough to enter through the gates of heaven. There are some people who will go as far as trying to distinguish one sin from another in terms of severity level. Sin is *sin,* no "ifs," "ands," or "buts" about it.

Here is something to think about: It is hard for a person to throw a rock at a glass house when the glass has already been shattered (let that marinate). It's hard for someone to shoot you down if you take the ammunition out of his gun (let that marinate, too). We won't be able to control those who constantly find joy in casting stones at others. However, we can slow their efforts by casting a stone at ourselves.

In order to cast a stone at yourself, you have to examine yourself to uncover the stone. Lamentations 3:40 says, "Let us search out and examine our ways, and turn back to the Lord." When you uncover the stone, present it to God through a prayer of forgiveness so it can be wiped away and you can get back in line with His will. In summary, don't be afraid to cast your own stone. It is better that you do it than someone else.

21

DON'T WORRY, EVERYTHING WILL BE ALRIGHT AND WILL WORK OUT FOR YOU

Romans 8:28

While I was unpacking my bag after arriving at work, the Holy Spirit said, "Don't worry, everything will be alright and will work out for you." What a mighty word to hear before starting my workday. With everything going on in my life at this appointed time, a word of reassurance is definitely needed.

How many of you know that *all* things work for your good? How many of you have been through something, thought it wasn't going to work out, but then it worked out in *your* favor? How many of you have worried (or are worrying) yourself sick because you weren't sure how things were going to work out, but then they worked out in *your* favor? Today, worry no more because everything will be alright. It's working out for you!

You may be going through something right now and feel ready to give up. You may be going through something right now and feel ready to walk away from it all. You may be going through something right now and feel like you don't have the strength to keep going. Don't give up! Don't walk away! Keep going! Though you may not see it right now, it's working for you!

You may be worrying about how your bills will get paid with the little money that you make or have in your bank account. You may be worrying because you have yet to find a new job because your current job is being eliminated (my own testimony). You may be worrying because you, a family member, or a friend has been stricken with sickness. You may be worrying because you can't quite understand why those close to you are causing you pain and why you are you inflicting pain upon them (it goes both ways). You may be worrying because it seems like you are always the one who gets the short end of the stick while those who do less than you are getting blessed. Regardless of the situation, don't worry because everything will be alright; it's working for you!

You are probably saying, "It is easy for you to say when you don't know what I am going through." And you know what? You are exactly right! I don't know what you are going through, but when you believe in God and know what God has done for you, then you can encourage others not to worry and know it is working for you! See, our problem is that we want to stand on faith when it is convenient for us or when our days are bright. But when our days are dark or grey, we can't find faith to stand on and walk around like a lost person in a dark house with no power during the storm who is stumbling over everything (let that marinate).

So today, my brothers and sisters, let go of that worrying spirit and activate your faith. Turn your worry into worship! Turn your pity into praise! You may be tired, but you will be blessed! You may want to give up, but don't give up because your labor is not in vain and you *will* reap your blessing in due time! You may have endured sleepless nights, but now it is time to rest! You may have cried tears of pain, but they will now be tears of joy! You may not see how it is going to work out, but it *is* working out!

If God did it before, surely, He can and *will* do it again! Today, the pity party ends! Today, the spirits of worry and depression will flee from you! Today, peace will enter your heart, mind, and spirit! Today, you will regain your confidence and your strength and will press forward! Today, you will acknowledge that if God didn't think you couldn't handle what you are in, then He would not allow you to be in it in the first place! He brought you to it and will lead you through it! It is working in your favor!

Today and moving forward, you don't have to worry because it's working for you!

Related Reading

1 Corinthians 15:58; Galatians 6:9; Philippians 4:6

YOU HAVE FAVOR

Exodus 33:13

How many times has a door been shut in your face but God opened a new door for you? How many times have you wondered how you were going to pay your bills but God made a way? How many times were you able to pay your bills on time when you didn't have a job because God made a way? How many times when you couldn't see your way out of a storm did God shine His light down on your storm and bring you out? How many times have you thought your situation was bad but God worked it out for your good? You have favor!

See, God blesses us with favor even when we don't deserve it. Do you think you are still here because of what you have done? Do you think you are still here due to your efforts? You are still here thanks to God's favor upon your life. You didn't get in trouble with your friends because of God's favor. You made it home safely after drinking heavily without a scratch because of God's favor. You were protected when you were having "unprotected fun" with no traces of anything because of God's favor.

You have been able to survive the trials and tribulations in your job, not because of your own will but God's favor. You don't look like what you have been through thanks to God's favor. What you thought was a temporary setback set you up for your blessing: God's favor. If you don't think you have favor, you better think again; think back to all those things you have done but can't explain because you don't know how it worked in your favor. Nothing but God's favor.

Because you have favor, you should (always) continue to seek God. Moses had the right prayer when he asked God, if he had found grace (favor) in His sight, to show him His way so he would know Him and find more grace (favor) in His sight. It is as if Moses was acknowledging that God had given him favor and that he wanted to receive more favor. There is nothing wrong with wanting more from God. The Word does say that He can do exceedingly abundantly above all we can ask or think according to the power that works in us (Eph. 3:20).

I am thankful for the favor God has shown me, but I will continue to seek after Him so He can bless me with more favor! We should all be thankful for God's favor. We should all be thankful that, even when we fall short, He blesses anyway! We should all be thankful that He looks beyond our faults, sees our needs, and blesses us anyway! We should all be thankful that, even when we don't deserve it, He blesses us anyway!

You have favor!

Related Reading

Romans 8:28

YOU DON'T LOOK LIKE WHAT YOU HAVE BEEN THROUGH

Exodus 3:2; Daniel 3:27

The Scriptures referenced above involved fire. The bush was on fire, but it was not consumed by the fire. Shadrach, Meshach, and Abed-Nego were placed in a fiery furnace but came out unharmed. In life, we go through some "fiery" situations. As a matter of fact, someone may be in a "fiery" situation right now! When we are in the fire, we may feel the heat of the fire, but the heat does not harm us. By God's grace and mercy, we are not consumed by the fire! Because of God's grace and mercy, there is *no* evidence of the fire upon us! No one will ever know about the fire you have been through unless you tell them about the fire you have been through (let that marinate)!

My brothers and sisters, you have been battered, beaten, and torn. You may even be going through a storm at this very moment that is tossing you around like a doll. You may be going through several situations that may be pulling you every way but loose. You may be in the midst of a circumstance that seems like pure hell. But despite what you have been through or what you are going through, you still look the same! You look good!

You lost friends and relationships, but you don't look like what you've been through! Your health has been attacked, your body racking with pain, but you don't look like what you've been through! You lost your job, your car, your home, but you don't look like what you've been through! You heart has been broken, your dreams shattered, your hope lost, but you don't look like what you've been through!

I thank God that I survived! My frown has been replaced with a smile! The tears of sadness are now tears of joy! The anger has been replaced with joy! My head does not hang low but is held high in giving God praise for bringing me through! I didn't like going through, but I thank God for going through! Because I went through, I have a greater appreciation for His grace! Because I went through, my faith is stronger! Because I went through, I am better than before! Because I went through, He is doing a new thing in my life! Victory is here because we went through! Breakthrough is here because we went through! Deliverance is here because we went through! Restoration is here because we went through! He is blessing you because you went through!

Can you imagine how we would look if not for God's grace? We would be a hot mess! Thank God for His grace! It is God's grace that covers our battle scars! It is God's grace that hides our spiritual bruises! It is God's grace that shields what we've been through from the world! It is God's grace that we don't look like what we have been through!

My brothers and sisters, you should smile and give God your best praise because you don't look like what you have been through or what you are going through!

IT'S SPIRITUAL

2 Corinthians 10:3-5

Have you wondered why, when something was going on in your life, it felt like you were spinning your wheels instead of making progress? Have you ever wondered why, no matter what you did in a situation, it didn't get better but seemed to get worse? Let me help you out! It's not a worldly thing. It's a spiritual thing!

It's spiritual! If Satan can show up in the wilderness to tempt Jesus, you best believe he will show up or send his demons to show up where the Word of God resides to battle against you! If Satan can enter the serpent and convince Eve to consume fruit from the tree of the knowledge of good and evil, then you best believe that he or his demons will enter a weak vessel (sometimes someone close to you) to attack you! If Satan showed up in the garden of Eden, then what makes you think he won't show up on your job, in your house, in your child's school? Wake up! Wake up! Wake up!

Wake up and understand that what you are going through is spiritual warfare, and spiritual warfare *cannot* be fought with a worldly mindset. It would be ludicrous for a soldier to take a knife to a war being fought with guns! If you go into a fight unprepared, then prepare to be defeated. I'm just saying! In order to fight the battle, you have to understand the battle.

The battles you are facing at work are not of this world; it's spiritual! The issues you are dealing with in your home are not of this world; it's spiritual! The things your child may be going through at school or the sudden changes you've seen in your child are not of this world; it's spiritual! As soon as the battle starts, we want to come out of our corner swinging and burn out very quickly. We burn out quickly because we are trying to fight a spiritual battle with a worldly mindset.

Call me "super spiritual" if you want. I will walk *proudly* with an "S" on my chest so the enemy will know that the fight will not be easy. The Word reminds us that we should put on the whole armor of God. It never said at any point that we should take it off (let that marinate). See, our problem is we want to put on the armor of God when we are in a battle and take it off when the sun is shining bright! You can't take it off! It has to stay on at *all* times! Why? The enemy does not take a vacation, coffee breaks, or a leave of absence! The enemy does not clock in and out! He works 24/7 every day! There may be breaks in a worldly battle, but a spiritual battle does not comprehend the concept of breaks. It is continuous. Because it is continuous, we must continue to wear the armor of God at *all* times!

It's spiritual! Do not ignore the signs! Do not be ignorant to Satan's devices! Oh, stop talking *about* your battle and start speaking *to* your battle (let that marinate)! We want to talk about how rough it is or how stressed we are, which gives power and life to the enemy! Your words are keeping the enemy on life support, so if you kill your words, then you will kill the enemy (let that marinate)! You can weaken the battle by speaking to the battle!

David didn't bow down to Goliath but spoke boldly to the giant by saying:

> *"You come to me with a sword, with a spear, and with a javelin but I come to you in the name of the Lord of hosts, the God of the armies, who you have defied. This day the Lord will deliver you into my hand, and I will strike you and take your head from you" (1 Sam. 17:45-46a).*

Check what you say in battle (let that marinate)! As a matter fact, let's speak it now! "Satan, you come to me with your games and wicked ways to bring me down, but I stand before you in the name of the Lord, the Lord, strong and mighty, who will deliver you into my hand!"

The battle is not yours; it's the Lord's. 2 Chronicles 20:17 says, "You will not *need* to fight in this *battle*. Position yourselves, stand still and see the salvation of the Lord, who is with you, O Judah and Jerusalem!" You are in the battle; stay in the battle! God is with you always! He will never leave you nor forsake you! And remember, what you are in is not of this world. It's spiritual!

Related Reading

Ephesians 6:12

YOUR STORY IS NOT OVER

John 11:23-26

The Holy Spirit spoke a word as I was driving to the office and had me shouting even when I sat down at my desk! The Holy Spirit said,

"Your story is *not* over!" Mind you, the "not" was not a simple "not" but stated emphatically! When they crucified Jesus and placed Him in the tomb, they thought His story was over, but it was only the beginning. They did not fully comprehend the Son of God and His obedience to His Father's will! They thought when He took His last breath that He was dead! *But* three days later, He rose from what they thought was going to be His final resting place!

Let's go back to the time before the crucifixion and resurrection of Jesus. When Lazarus died, Martha said to Jesus in John 11:21, "Lord, if You had been here my brother would not have died!" I would bet that she did not understand that Lazarus had to die and remain in that state for a few days so God could be glorified! Do you see the relation? Jesus died and remained in His state for three days, and God was glorified through His resurrection. Jesus assured Martha that Lazarus would rise again.

Martha said, "I know he will rise in the resurrection!" She thought the resurrection was an event like a birthday, Mother's Day, Father's Day, etc. But see, the resurrection was not an event but a person! The resurrection is Jesus! Jesus said (with my emphasized interpretation), "I am the resurrection and the life. He who believes in *me*, though he may die, he *shall* live!"

My brothers and sisters, you may be walking in some stormy weather that you think is going to take you out, but your story is *not* over! You may be hurting right now and ready to give up, but don't give up because your story is *not* over! Your situation (i.e. job, family, marriage, health, finances, etc.) may appear to be dead or is dead, but your story is *not* over! You may feel like it's over, but please know that it is *not!* Your story is not over because we serve a risen Savior who has the power to resurrect our situations! Your story is not over because, at the right time, Jesus will step in to resurrect your situation for God's glory! Your story is not over because His story never ended (let that marinate)!!!

My brothers and sisters, be encouraged and stay encouraged! Through the heartache and pain, keep pushing! Just as they were amazed when Jesus wasn't in the tomb, you will be amazed when our amazing Savior resurrects your situation. You will rise! Your situation will rise! Your situation shall live and will live! This is only the beginning!

Your story is *not* over!!!

Related Reading

Mark 16:6-8

ARE YOU WILLING FOR HIS GLORY?

Genesis 22:1-2, 11-14

This account of Abraham and his relationship with God is powerful, as it demonstrates Abraham's obedience to God's command and what he was willing to do for God's glory. We are placed in various situations or go through storms that will test our obedience. If you tell God, "For your glory, I will do anything," you better believe your words will be tested (let that marinate).

From the text, it appears that Abraham did not question God's command or hesitate to fulfill the order. How many times have we received a command and questioned it? How many times have we received a command and hesitated in our action to fulfill the command? Better yet, how many times have we received a command and didn't do what we were told *at all?* Our faithfulness should drive our obedience to fulfill *any* command spoken into our lives by God.

Abraham's action shows a strong respect or reverence for God. It also shows that Abraham believed if he sacrificed his son for God, God could resurrect his son as a result of his obedience and faith (testing the tester). Let me throw this in; if God asks you to sacrifice something or someone, then do it with faith in knowing that He can resurrect the very thing He is asking you to sacrifice.

Remember, Job was blessed with more in his latter days than his former. As some like to say, Job was blessed with double for his trouble! Now ponder on this. It's ironic that we see a father willing to sacrifice his son in the Old Testament and our Father sacrifice His Son in the New Testament. From this, I would say that God would not ask us to do something that He is not willing to do Himself (my God, let that marinate for real)!

The beauty of Abraham's willingness to be obedient and sacrifice his son was not only acknowledged by God, but provision was made for the sacrifice: a ram in the bush. Abraham was willing to sacrifice his son, so what are you willing to sacrifice at God's command? The willingness to be obedient may come with a lack of understanding as to why He has asked you to do something.

You may not understand why He asked you to turn in your resignation. You may not understand why He asked you to pay your tithes with the last little bit of money in your account. You may not understand why He allowed you to endure heartache and pain. You may not understand why He allowed things and people to be taken from you.

When it is for His glory, we will not comprehend it. When it is for His glory, we will not be comfortable. When it is for His glory, we have to trust Him regardless. Through the hurt and pain, trust Him! Through the losses, trust Him! Through the disappointments, trust Him! Through it all, trust Him!

When we are going through a storm, He will provide! When we are standing in need, He will provide! Obedience, however, is the key! When we are obedient to His command, He will provide! Deuteronomy 28:1-14 speaks of the blessings we can receive through our obedience to God's command. He will make you the head and not the tail through your obedience! He will put you above and not beneath through your obedience! He will make you a lender and not a borrower through your obedience! In order to receive the blessings He has for us, we have to follow Abraham's example and be obedient to Him. Obedience will always produce a ram in the bush!

For His glory, are you willing to do anything? Think about it, pray about it, and let it marinate!

HANDLE YOUR KINGDOM BUSINESS

Haggai 1:3-11

Have you ever wondered why it took so long to receive a blessing? Have you ever wondered why others were experiencing a season of blessing while you were experiencing a drought? Are you handling your Kingdom business?

Maybe God has not rained down blessings in your life because you haven't put His business first. Maybe you are going through hell in the workplace because you are not putting your Kingdom purpose first. Maybe you haven't been blessed financially because you haven't been a good steward over the little you've received nor given God what's due Him (I can testify on this one—let that marinate). Maybe you haven't been blessed with more because you are complaining about the little you have when you should be thanking God for what you have. Maybe you haven't been blessed with a spouse or strong relationship because of the weak relationship you have with God. We can go on and on; the question remains: are you handling your Kingdom business?

From my personal experience, I can definitely relate to the account in Haggai. When I didn't put God first or handle my Kingdom business, I felt it! But when I put my Kingdom business first, I would reap the rewards of my work. I heard a rap artist by the name of "Dee-1" say in a television interview that God told him that He wanted to elevate him to have a platform of millions, but God wanted to make sure his walk for Him was righteous.

Dee-1 testified that one of his areas that was difficult in being righteous was remaining celibate before marriage. He knew that if he could conquer the difficulty of being celibate, then he would have a platform of millions. He said millions of people are watching the show! God is blessing Dee-1 as a result of him putting his Kingdom business first! His testimony not only blessed me but served as a reminder that when you put your Kingdom business first, blessings will come!

In order to know what your Kingdom business is, you must seek God. Matthew 6:33 says, "But seek first the kingdom of God and His righteousness, and all these things shall be added to you." Everyone has a Kingdom purpose! It is left up to us to seek God to receive our Kingdom purpose. Once we receive our Kingdom purpose, then we should start operating in our Kingdom purpose! We should start working in it. We should be about our Father's Kingdom business. The season you are experiencing may not have anything to do with the enemy attacking you. Rather, it may be a result of you slacking in handling your Kingdom business! If you take care of the Father, then our Father *will* take care of you! Handle your Kingdom business!!

GET READY FOR THE SHIFT

Ezekiel 37:7-10

For a moment, place yourself in Ezekiel's shoes in the midst of the valley surrounded by bones. God commands you to speak to the bones. As you speak, the bones begin to shift and move! As you speak, the bones start to come together! As you speak, what was once dead is now coming alive! What appeared as a bunch of scattered bones, a bunch of mess, a dead situation is coming together, grand and alive!

Just like Ezekiel, many of us are in a valley of dry bones, but the difference between Ezekiel and us is that we are *not* speaking to shift our dry bones. We are talking about the dry bones but not speaking *to* the dry bones (let that marinate)! We are not speaking to shift the atmosphere of our valley experience! We are not praising to shift the atmosphere of our valley experience! We are not worshipping the One who can shift the atmosphere of our valley experience!

Instead of speaking life into our valley experience, we continue to speak death (i.e. "I can't," "I will never," words of discouragement or a lack of faith). Instead of praising in our valley experience, we are holding pity parties and inviting anyone who is willing to join us! Instead of worshipping in our valley experience, we are worrying and discouraging others who are watching us go through our experience from going through their own experience (really let that marinate)!

We say that we have faith but fail to exercise our faith in the times it is needed most. Everyone has faith when times are good, but where is your faith when times are hard? Where is your faith when you have been given an unfavorable report from the doctor? Where is your faith when a loved one or spouse walks away from you? Where is your faith when you've been told that you will no longer have a job after committing to your employer for years?

Ezekiel exercised his faith when God asked him if the bones could live, and he responded, "O Lord God, You know." We want our situation to change but don't exercise our faith to change our situation or exercise our faith to believe in the One who can change our situation! We want to experience a shift but don't shift our faith into position to experience a shift!

God will give you what you need to shift your situation! Ezekiel was listening to God and did as He commanded. God told Ezekiel what to speak, and Ezekiel spoke it. Oh, but in order to listen to God and do as He commands, you have to be in a position to hear and have a relationship with Him (let that marinate).

What I love about Ezekiel and his dry bones experience is the end. He started out looking at a bunch of bones. After he prophesied to the bones, the bones came together, and an exceedingly great army stood before him. If you are not shouting because of that, then let me help you. Ezekiel started with something that didn't look like much but ended with a great army! If you believe just a little bit, God will exceed it. Now to Him who is able to do exceedingly abundantly above all that we ask or think, according to the power that works in us (Eph. 3:20)! Can I give you something else to shout about? "'The glory of this latter temple shall be greater that the former,' says the Lord of hosts. 'And in this place I will give peace, says the Lord of hosts'" (Hag. 2:9).

My brothers and sisters, your "dry bones" are not dead! Your finances are not dead! Your marriage is not dead! Your job is not a dead-end situation! Whatever your situation may be at this time, it is not dead! The pieces of your broken heart *will* be restored! Joy *will* be restored! Peace *will* be restored! Love *will* be restored! You can shift your situation!

Yokes will be destroyed! Chains will be destroyed, not broken because broken things can be put back together (let that marinate)! You will experience your breakthrough! You will be delivered! You will see life in your situation! You *will* experience a move of God, but the shift starts with you. Stop complaining and start praising! Stop fussing and start praying! Stop pouting and start worshipping! When you shift your ways to fall in line with His ways, you will shift *you* out of the way and let God have His way, and your situation will shift!

It's time for a shift, and I am ready for the shift! Get ready! Your shift is on the way!

FOR HIS GLORY: IT BELONGS TO HIM

Romans 11:36

As I was sitting at my desk, a heavy spirit came upon me, and I began to ask the Lord, "Why?" Don't get super spiritual and say I shouldn't be asking why. Sometimes, you have to ask why to understand the why (let that marinate). The response was clear and straight forward. It came through the next song in my playlist. "For My Glory!" The Holy Spirit guided me to John 11:4. "When Jesus heard *that*, He said, 'This sickness is not unto death, but for the glory of God, that the Son of God may be glorified through it.'" The Holy Spirit said your pain is for His glory! Your tears are for His glory! Your heartache is for His glory! Your rejection is for His glory! What you go through is for His glory!

Simply put, *all* the glory belongs to God! Whatever you may be going through, He gets the glory! Your body may be racking with pain, but He gets the glory! Your bank account may be low or out of order, but He gets the glory! *All* the glory belongs to Him! You may be mistreated on your job, but He gets the glory! People have turned their backs to you, but He gets the glory! The doctor has given you an unfavorable report, but He gets the glory! He wakes us up in the morning!

All the glory belongs to Him! He keeps us in our right minds! *All* the glory belongs to Him! We have breath in our bodies every morning! All the glory belongs to Him! We are not consumed by our storms! All the glory belongs to Him! We don't look like what we have been through! All the glory belongs to Him! With all that He does, all the glory belongs to Jesus! Nobody on this earth deserves the glory due to Him. All the glory belongs to God! Though the enemy may slay me, yet I will trust in Him! *All* the glory belongs to God! In *all* things, all the glory belongs to God!

Every time I open my eyes, God gets the glory! Every time I take a breath, God gets the glory! When I have gone through crazy situations, stressful situations, painful situations but am still in my right mind, God gets the glory! When others let me down and He picks me up, God gets the glory! There is no shame in the glory that I give God! In my home, God gets the glory! In my car, God gets the glory! On my job, God gets the glory! He is the Author and the Finisher, the Beginning and the End, the Provider and the Sustainer, the Healer and the Comforter! He is our everything.

We may not understand what God is doing, but it is for His glory! We may not like what God is doing or allowing to happen in our lives, but it is for His glory! Your next move may be scary, but it is for His glory! You may be experiencing hard times, but it is for His glory! Your life may be uncomfortable at the moment, but it is for His glory! The question is will you do anything for His glory? Will you do whatever it takes for His glory? Will you do what He asks of you for His glory?

I may not understand what God is doing right now or be able to see what God is doing right now, but I have to believe that what He is doing in this season is *for His glory!* You may not understand what God is doing right now or be able to see what God is doing right now in your situation, but you have to believe that what He is doing is *for His glory!*

My brothers and sisters, stay encouraged! It is for His glory, and the glory belongs to Him!

Related Reading

Lamentations 3:22-24

YOUR "YES" WILL BE CHALLENGED

Matthew 4:1-11

In this familiar account, Jesus was led to the wilderness to be tempted by Satan. The first verse alone is confirmation that Satan will not always lead you to temptation. You may be led by the Holy Spirit to temptation to test your stamina, your strength, and your faith in dealing with the temptation (let that marinate). With each temptation, Jesus didn't respond with words that sounded good, an attitude, or a defeated mindset. He responded with the Word of God.

Our (man) words speak life to our storms, temptations, etc., but speaking the Word of God will take away the little power of our storm, temptations, etc. (let that marinate, too). Oh! Let me also point out to some and remind others that Satan knows the Word but will omit part of the Word to get to you. In verse 6, Satan says to Him, "If You are the Son of God, throw Yourself down. For it is written; '*He shall give His angels charge over you,*' and, '*In their hands they shall bear you up, lest you dash your foot against a stone.*'" I won't reveal what was omitted in his statement but will leave it to you to study the Word for yourself to find the omission and help build you up in the Word. After the failed attempts, Satan left Jesus.

Jesus said "yes" to God's will for His life. He was challenged in the wilderness, and Luke's account serves as a reminder that Satan will continue to challenge us from time to time. My brothers and sisters, we should understand and embrace the fact that when we say "yes" to Jesus, our "yes" will be challenged. Our "yes" will be challenged to test our faith. Our "yes" will be challenged to test our allegiance to Jesus. Our "yes" will be challenged to test our strength. Our "yes" will be challenged to prepare us for the next level or next stop in our journey.

Your finances will be challenged! Your friendships will be challenged! Your family will be challenged! Your marriage will be challenged! Your patience will be challenged! Your prayer life will be challenged!

Your peace will be challenged! You will face challenges at home! You will face challenges at work! You will face challenges at school! You will face challenges everywhere! When you face your challenge, don't lean on yourself to deal with it. Take up the whole armor of God so that you may be able to withstand the evil of that day, and having done all, stand in faith! When you face your challenge, stand boldly before it just like David when he stood boldly before Goliath and defeated him through faith. Stand on the Word! Stand on His promise! Just stand!

The Word of God does not promise that our days will be easy. The Word of God does not promise that our acceptance of the Savior will be easy. Your "yes" *will be* challenged, so get ready, get ready, get ready! Remember, you are *more* than a conqueror and no weapon formed against you shall prosper! Your "yes" will be challenged, but you will *not* be defeated by the challenge!

Related Reading

Luke 4:13

ANOINTED ATTITUDE

Joshua 1:3-5, 9

I would contend that we serve a very strategic God. A chess master thinks strategically before making a move. As a matter of fact, a chess master not only thinks about his or her current move but considers the 3 or 4 moves after the current one (let that marinate). God has a strategic purpose for our lives and strategically places us where He wants us to be as part of His strategic plan.

I used to question why I was placed in certain situations, why I am working where I am working, why I am living where I am living, etc. I will be very transparent; my attitude was not what it is today. Instead of understanding why I was where I was, I was trying to get out of what I was in (let that marinate). At one point in my career, I was dissatisfied with my position at work and was looking for opportunities to get out of the role. The Holy Spirit spoke to me and said, "When you humble yourself in your current role, you will be positioned for your next role" (let that marinate).

When I received this word, my eyes were opened to the fact I was being positioned for ministry to go forth through me but was too busy thinking about myself (selfish). Once I accepted my purpose, my attitude changed! Now, don't get me wrong. I still experience bad days, but the days are not as bad as before. My attitude changed from bad to anointed.

God told Joshua that everywhere he walked would be given to him. When Moses was on top of Mount Nebo, God allowed him to see all the land promised to the children of Israel. Joshua was anointed to continue what God started through Moses. Moses was anointed to lead the children of Israel out of Egypt, and Joshua was anointed to take the children into the promised land. Joshua and Moses had an anointed purpose. *You* have an anointed purpose! When you discover, understand, embrace, and activate your purpose, you should take on an Anointed Attitude!

See, when I embraced my calling and purpose, especially in the workplace, I realized God anointed me with a purpose. I am anointed for this! You are anointed for this! When I looked back on my work situation and realized that others would not have been able to do what I did, I knew it was nobody but God and the anointing He gave me. With an anointed attitude, I can remind myself, "I am *anointed!*" With an anointed attitude, I can encourage myself, "I am *anointed!*"

With an anointed attitude, I believe that everything I touch will be blessed! With an anointed attitude, I believe that everything I lay my eyes on will be blessed! With an anointed attitude, I believe any mistreatment of the anointing will cause others to miss out on the blessing of the anointing (let that marinate)! With an anointed attitude, you are blessed because He has blessed you with me; this is not conceit but an understanding that God is using this broken vessel to be a blessing to others and can use you in the same manner.

You are where you are for a reason! God will not allow us to be somewhere if we cannot handle it. God will not allow us to go through something if He doesn't have faith in us to go through it! You are in your position at work because you are anointed to be in it! You are going through the fire because you are anointed to handle it! You are where you are in life because you are anointed to be where you are! When the enemy starts playing with your emotions, remind the enemy, "I am *anointed!*" Oh, let this quote marinate in your spirit: "*Attitudes are contagious. Do you want people around you to catch yours?*" -Bob Moawad. Your anointed attitude can edify or help others in ways unknown to you.

You are *anointed*, so act like it! You are anointed for this, so act like it! You have an anointed attitude, so *use it!*

UPGRADE YOUR ATTITUDE

James 4:6, 10

I've heard it said, "Upgrade your attitude so you can upgrade your altitude." Maybe the reason why your plane hasn't taken off is because your attitude is keeping you grounded. Maybe the reason why you haven't experienced the change you desire is because you haven't changed the attitude you exhibit. Maybe the reason why you haven't grown in your career is because of your attitude of entitlement! Maybe the reason why you are not moving forward is because your attitude is holding you back.

In order to receive something, we may be required to give up or sacrifice something. The Word says that God resists the proud but gives grace to the humble. Now who doesn't want more grace? I am not too proud to say that I want more of what God has for me and will give up what I need to give up in order to receive what He has for me. We can't expect to be blessed with the same attitude.

Insanity is doing the same thing over and over again and expecting different results. We can't maintain the same attitude all the time and expect different results. We have to change our attitudes to see different results. *You* have to decide whether or not *your* attitude will change! If you are not willing to change, then don't get upset when others are being blessed as a result of their changed attitudes!

A bad attitude is like a flat tire. If you don't change it, you'll never go anywhere!

Upgrade Your Attitude!!

FORGIVE AND BE FORGIVEN

Mark 11:25-26

The Lord's prayer is perhaps the first prayer we learn as a child. We learn how to recite the words but are not given a true understanding of the power of the prayer. We recite a prayer that sounds good but truly do not understand how good it is for us. Though this next statement may come with some criticism or backlash, I will say it boldly. Over time, we recite a vain prayer, an empty prayer; a powerless prayer. In my opinion, it's almost as if we say the Lord's prayer because we were taught to say it, again, without understanding the power of it.

In the Lord's prayer, we are asking the Father to forgive us as we forgive others. "But it is hard to forgive someone who did you wrong." "It is hard to forgive someone who left you hanging." "It is hard to forgive someone who walked away from you." "It is hard to forgive myself for the things I have done." "It is hard to forgive." These are some common phrases, or better yet, excuses, we say in terms of forgiveness.

The root word of forgiveness is "forgive," and I define it as "to stop feeling anger toward someone" or "stop feeling anger about something." Our inability or unwillingness to forgive becomes a burden which weighs heavily in our spirit. In some instances, our unwillingness to forgive hinders our progression, our growth. It takes a toll, not only on us but those connected to us, as they feel the effects (attitude, stress, sickness, etc.) of our unwillingness to forgive. As much as we try not to forgive others, we courageously go to the Lord in prayer and seek forgiveness of our sins.

Why are you holding on to something that happened years ago? Why are you holding on to something that really didn't have anything to do with you? Why are you angry with someone who is not even thinking about you? Why are you losing sleep because you are mad at someone who lays his or her head down every night and gets a good night's rest? Whatever or whomever you are not willing to forgive, is it really worth it?

If you were looking for a quick feel-good word, you can stop now because this is not it. This is a healing word, and we have some wounds overdue for a good healing! Healing comes through forgiveness. Jesus said, "But if you do not forgive, neither will your Father in heaven forgive your trespasses." The Word does not have to be manipulated or twisted for us to understand that we are held accountable to forgive. In order to be forgiven, we must first forgive. Forgive and live (let that marinate)!

Related Reading

Matthew 6:12

BE GRATEFUL AND BE BLESSED

Matthew 25:23

Have you ever wondered why it took a long time for you to receive a blessing? Have you ever wondered why you had to go through what you went through before you were blessed with your blessing? After receiving your blessing, have you ever looked back at the journey leading to your blessing? I used to question God and ask why it was taking so long to be blessed or why I was going through certain circumstances to get to my blessing. At one point in my life, I became frustrated because I would see everyone else being blessed except me. It wasn't until the Holy Spirit set me straight in "my ways" and "my thinking" that I understood why.

This next statement may rub someone the wrong way or understandably incite disagreement. We don't receive our blessing until we are mature enough to receive it. This was an eye opener when it was revealed to me. We don't receive our blessing until He deems us ready to receive it. Let's be honest. Sometimes, we truly do not embrace our blessings. Instead of appreciating what or whom we have in our lives, we focus on what or whom we don't have and desire to have.

We want to be blessed with a promotion but don't appreciate and embrace our current positions; we complain instead of giving praise. We want to be blessed with a husband or wife but don't appreciate and embrace our season of singleness; period, that should be spent with God (let that marinate). We want to be blessed financially but don't appreciate God by giving back a portion of what *He* made possible for us to receive (definitely let that marinate, too).

How can we expect God to bless us with more when we don't appreciate what little we have in our possession? So, if God gives us a blessing before our time to receive, we may not be ready for it. If He gives us a blessing before our time, we may mess it up. We have to go through a preparation period to not only get us ready to *receive* our blessing but to *appreciate* it.

Big or small, blessings are blessings, and we should be grateful for all that is bestowed upon us. Honestly speaking, we don't deserve 95% of the blessings we receive, but God blesses us anyway. That alone is reason to praise and worship Him! Even though we fall short of His glory, He blesses us anyway! We should not take our blessings for granted; appreciate your blessings *now* and not when they are gone!

We can't expect God to bless us with more if we are not thankful for less. When you humble yourself to embrace and appreciate your blessings in your current position, then you will be positioned to receive more blessings. "God resists the proud but gives grace to the humble" (James 4:6b).

Be grateful and be blessed!

Related Reading

Luke 16:10; James 4:10

GOD WILL NEVER

Psalm 37:23-24

For those of you who may be in the midst of a storm, this is for you. When someone is down, I would contend that we don't do enough to edify him or help build him up. We would rather see a person stay down in her storm versus stand strong in her storm! I pray these words do more than just make you feel good but also minister to your spirit and give you the encouragement to get up and keep pressing forward!

God will *never* let you down! As you are going through, remember that you serve a God who will never let you down! The Message translation of 1 Corinthians 10:13 reminds us that God will never let us down and will always be there to help us come through! Man will let you down, but God will never let you down!

God will *never* leave you! God told Joshua that He would never leave nor forsake him and that He would be with him just as He was with Moses. The same applies to you! Even when you think you are alone, God is with you!

God will *never* lie to you! As the Scripture (Num. 23:19a) says, "God is not a man that He should lie!" In Isaiah, we are reminded that His Word will never return to Him void. Not only will God never lie to you, but He will never lie to Himself when He speaks things into and over our lives! God will never break a promise made to Himself (let that marinate)!

God will *never* let you stay down when you fall! When you stumble and fall, God will not leave you lying down. He will pick you up so you can keep going. Only you can decide whether or not you stay down after a fall (really let that marinate)!

God will *never* break your heart! If anything, your broken heart is God's opportunity to let His glory refract on your brokenness so it can be seen by all (let that marinate)!

God will *never* let you go! There is an old song that encourages us to hold on to God's unchanging hand! God is the same yesterday, today, and will be the same forever. Even when *we* change, He doesn't change! Even when *we* let go of Him, He will never let go of us! His hand is *always* on us! I like to call His hands "Grace" and "Mercy," for it was His Grace and Mercy that kept me when I didn't keep Him near me (let that marinate)!

If I could hold a tune, I would sing, "Never would have made it, never would have made it without You!" My brothers and my sisters, we would have never made it this far if not for our God! I am thankful that God is not like man and will never do what man will do (let that marinate). It is my prayer that those of you who are going through find comfort, strength, and support in these words. Even if you are not going through, may the Holy Spirit bring back to your remembrance this word as a source of encouragement, and may it bless you in your season.

Related Reading

Joshua 1:5b; Psalm 34:18; Isaiah 55:11; 1 Corinthians 10:13 (MSG); Hebrews 13:8

WON'T HE DO IT

Isaiah 55:11

As I was meditating during my morning commute, the Holy Spirit would not let me wallow in my storm! Instead, the Holy Spirit had me focus on the One standing with me in the storm! The Holy Spirit said, "You are like an oak tree in a storm. You are bending, but you won't break! The stress of your storm hurts, but the restoration will be greater than the pain!" The first thing that came to my mind was "won't He do it!"

My brothers and sisters, God will always do what He says He will do! Do you remember your last storm? Of course! You do because you are still here to remember it! If He did it before, then, surely, He will do it *again!* My brothers and sisters, I want to encourage you and encourage myself to trust God as we go through our storm(s)! "He is able to do exceedingly abundantly above all that we ask or think, according to His power that works in and through us." If He says it, then it shall be! When He speaks, something happens! His word *never* returns to Him void! Won't He do it? Yes, He will!!

Be encouraged to stand in your storm! Be encouraged to stay in the fight! The battle is not yours but the Lord's! All we have to do is show up, stand still (surrender our ways to His ways), and watch God have His way in our storms! You best believe that when my storm is no more, I will praise Him and say, "Won't He do it!" You know what? Let me change my thinking! Death and life are in the power of the tongue, so let me correct myself! You best believe while I am *in* the storm, I will praise Him through my pain and say, "Won't He do it! Yes, He will!"

Believe it, declare it, receive it, and walk in it! Won't He do it!! Yes, my God will!!

Related Reading

2 Chronicles 20:15, 17; Ephesians 3:20

YOU ARE BUILT GOD-TOUGH!

Job 1:8-12; Isaiah 54:17

This is an encouraging word for those of you who may be going through something or simply need to be reminded of who you are and *Whose* you are! In the account of Job, Satan had to get permission to cause him harm. Even with permission, his actions or powers were limited, as he could not kill Job. *No weapon formed against me shall prosper* (let that marinate)! If you ever thought you had a bad day, Job *really* had a bad day. His children, riches, and all of his possessions were taken from him then his health was attacked. Does this sound familiar (let that marinate, too)? Though there is much more on the account of Job, all that he lost was restored in the end.

What are you saying? I'm glad you asked. God had faith in Job and offered him to Satan. I believe that God has the same faith in us and allows us to go through the things that we go through. Why? Because we are built God-tough! Job was anointed to go through what he went through; he was made for the trials and tribulations he faced. We have to understand or be reminded that we are made in the image of God, and since we are made or built in His image, we have the toughness to go through what He allows us to go through.

I strongly believe if Job wasn't built to go through what God allowed him to go through, then we would be reading a name other than Job! You are anointed to go through what you are going through! I am anointed to go through what I go through. We may not like what we are going through but have to trust God while we are going through because He is allowing us to go through!

If you are going through something, tell yourself, "I was built for this!" Tell yourself, "I can handle this!" Tell yourself, "If He gave me this, then I was made for this!" As we like to say, if God brings you to it, then He will bring you through it! Even Job said, "I know that You can do everything, and that no purpose *of Yours* can be withheld from You" (Job 42:2).

You are built with a purpose; you got this! You are built God-tough!!

YOUR WAY IS ON THE WAY

Exodus 14:16, 21-22

As the children of Israel were fleeing Pharaoh, they came upon the Red Sea. They were afraid because the enemy was upon them, and through their worldly eyes, there was nowhere to go. They began to panic and wish they were back in Egypt (some of us prefer to go back to or stay in the mess than deal with the process of getting out of the mess; let that marinate). Just when they thought they would perish, God made a way out of no way! He parted the Red Sea so the children could get to the other side, out of harm's way. Now get this! God used the "dead end" to bring an end to the trouble that was following His children (let that marinate). Thank you, Holy Spirit! God will bring you to the end of something dead and make a way so you can walk into something new (let that marinate, too)!

We have to trust God at all times! We cannot believe or accept a situation like a used car, "as is!" We have to stand on His Word and allow Him to handle the situation for us. Your back may be against the wall but *trust God!* You may feel like you are at rock bottom but trust The Solid Rock! You may feel as all hope is lost but *trust God!* You may feel like there is no way out but *trust God!* What may look like the end is really only the beginning (let that marinate)!

I am encouraging myself as I share this thought! You are going to make it! I am going to make it! We are going to make it! Through the pain, He will make a way! Through the tears, He will make a way! Through the stress, He will make a way! Through the roller coaster of emotions, I believe God *will* make a way for you and me! As the old folks would say, "Hold on just a little while longer; trouble don't last always!" So, my brothers and my sisters, you keep holding on! I am going to keep holding on!

In Jesus's name, I pray against the spirit of doubt, the spirit of fear, the spirit of stress, the spirit of depression, the spirit of anger, the spirit of hate, or any spirit not of God that attempts to influence you to let go of His unchanging hand. Those spirits will *not* win! We will not turn away from the King of kings and Lord of lords! We will stand strong and watch Him work! We are going to keep holding on to God's unchanging hand, and He *will* see us through! And when the way has been made, we will give God all the glory!

Your way is on the way!

IT WILL COME TO PASS

1 John 5:14-15

God wants to remind us that we should trust and believe in Him. Whatever we are going through *will* pass! Yes, you may be in the midst of a storm right now, but it *will* pass! Yes, you may be going through a hardship right now, but it *will* pass! Yes, your health may be under attack, but it *will* pass! Yes, you may be at a breaking point, but it *will* pass! Yes, you may be on the verge of losing your job, but it *will* pass! Yes, you may be dealing with an attack on your home, but it *will* pass! Yes, your family may be under attack, but it *will* pass. You've been in a wilderness situation for a long time, but it *will* pass!

God is not a God that will leave us when we need Him the most! God is not a God who will go back on His word! God will never fail you! Your momma can't do it! Your daddy can't do it! Your brothers or sisters can't do it! Big momma can't do it! Your friends can't do it! Dr. Phil can't do it! Oprah can't do it! Iyanla Vanzant can't do it! Buddha can't do it! Muhammad can't do it! Hennessy can't do it! Marijuana can't do it! But God can and *will* do exactly what He says He will do!

Stop and think about everything you went through before your current storm. He brought you through before, so He can bring you through what you are in right now. And if you are not in a storm at this present time, trust and believe that the promises He spoke in your life will come to pass!

Here is the key! You *have* to trust Him! I know you are experiencing pain and it hurts! I know you have been shedding tears and may not have any tears left to shed! But if you believe, you *have* to trust Him! Job said, "Though He slay me, yet I will trust in Him" (Job 13:15). Job made another powerful statement that I would contend is overlooked. He said, "If a man dies, shall he live again? All the days of my hard service I will wait, Till my change comes" (Job 14:14).

Through your storm, you *have* to wait on Him! Through your pain, you have to wait on Him! The Word says, "Wait on the Lord; be of good courage, and He shall strengthen your heart; Wait, I say, on the Lord" (Ps. 27:14). You can't hurry God! You have to wait on Him! He wants you to wait on Him! Wait on God; it will come to pass!

Whatever you need, trust and believe in the Lord! It *will* come to pass! Breakthrough? He's going to do it! Deliverance? He's going to do it! Healing? He's going to do it! Peace? He's going to do it! Promotion? He's going to do it! Increase? He's going to do it! Overflow? He's going to do it! God is right by your side! He said that He would never leave nor forsake us! He will see you through your situation! He will see you through your storm! Don't you give up but put your trust in the Lord! Don't bow down to your situation but bow down to God! Trust in the Lord! Believe in the Lord! Wait on the Lord! It *will* come to pass!!

Related Reading

Proverbs 3:5-6; Philippians 4:19

YOU WILL BE RESTORED

Joel 2:23-27

During my morning meditation, I heard the Holy Spirit say, "Restoration—you will be restored. Don't give in to your flesh but stand strong on your faith." It is always my prayer that I hear and receive what God is speaking to me. I know this is not just a word for me but at least one other person who is pushing through pain, enduring a storm. If it is you, I pray you find comfort in these words and are blessed by these words.

You have endured a lot. In the midst of your storm, you have lost some stuff. In the midst of your storm, you have lost some people. You tried to keep some things from going overboard as you were being tossed around but lost them. You've experienced losses in your finances, friendships, work, home, family, marriage, etc. Your peace, joy, happiness, strength, and love have gone overboard in your storm.

The things you lost were replaced with anger, pain, hurt, a broken heart, low self-esteem, depression, alcohol dependency, etc. You wanted to give up, but the little faith remaining in you would *not* let you let go! Despite your emotions, you recognized that God continues to bless you with undeserved grace and mercy, which has encouraged you to keep your faith! You have confessed your sins and asked for forgiveness.

If you have not confessed your sins, do so right now! Upon confession of your sins, say this quick prayer, "'Create in me a clean heart, O God, and renew a steadfast spirit within me. Do not cast me from

Your presence, and do not take Your Holy Spirit from me.' Amen" (Ps. 51:10-11, NIV). It is *never* too late to confess your sins!

My brothers and sisters, you *will* be restored! God is going to restore the things you've lost! I believe God will open the heavens and send an exceedingly abundant rain to you! With all I have endured, I believe God is going to restore me, and the blessings He will pour out from the windows of heaven will be so abundant that others will be blessed by my overflow! Let your faith, your praise, and your worship change the atmosphere in your life and make it conducive for God to rain in your life!

It may be a financial rain, a joyful rain, a loving rain, a healing rain, a strengthening rain; the rain God sends will be the rain that you need to restore what has been lost! As I share this thought with you, I am excited and giving thanks, not for restoration in my life but restoration that all of His faithful children will receive. See, I can rejoice for the restoration of others because if He will do it for them, then I know He will do it for me. Plus, it may not be my time for restoration, but I can sow into the restoration of others!

Galatians 6:8-10 says, "For he who sows to his flesh will of the flesh reap corruption, but he who sows to the Spirit will of the Spirit reap everlasting life. And let us not grow weary while doing good, for in due season we shall reap if we do not lose heart. Therefore, as we have opportunity, let us do good to all, especially to those who are of the household of faith." If I sow seeds of praise and worship into the restoration of others, then I will reap my restoration in due season (let that marinate)!

Hold on, my brothers and sisters! As you endure your storm, remember God is with you! Thank you, Holy Spirit! The Holy Spirit reminded me that this is not your first storm; He has restored you after the previous storms and will do the same after this storm! Your brokenness *will* be restored! Your joy *will* be restored! Your finances *will* be restored! Your family *will* be restored! Your peace *will* be restored! Your strength *will* be restored! Your marriage *will* be restored! Your health *will* be restored! Your losses *will* be restored!! Let me speak this into your life: "I see you in the future, and you look much better than you do right now!" You *will* be restored!!

Related Reading

Job 42:12

THE TOMB CAN'T HOLD YOU

Matthew 28:1-8

On July 30, 2014, I was blessed to deliver my initial sermon entitled "The Tomb Can't Hold You." Ironically, I found myself in a "tomb" four years later. If I am in a "tomb," then I know there is someone else who is also in a "tomb." Your tomb may be financial debt, stress, health-related, depression, marital issues, etc. It may feel like you can't get up, but you can and you *will!!* Your "tomb" can't hold you!

Every time I read the account of Jesus's crucifixion, I smile because they actually thought He would stay in the tomb and placed guards outside of the tomb so His body could not be removed. I smile because death could not hold Him down! I smile and shout because if death could not hold Him down, then nothing the enemy may try to do against you or me can hold us down!

Because He rose, I will rise above my circumstances! Because He rose, you will rise above your circumstances! Because He rose, I will rise above my storm! Because He rose, you will rise above your storm! Because He rose, I will rise!! Because He rose, you *will* rise! Jesus was not a prisoner of the tomb but a conqueror of the tomb! He rose from the very place tasked to keep Him down.

My brothers and sisters, my intent with this thought is not to give you false hope but to remind you that you are a child of God. If *the* Child of God rose from the tomb, there is no "tomb" that can hold you down unless you give it *your* authority to rule over you (let that marinate)!

When Jesus died and rose again, He won the victory for you and me! Because *He* won the victory, *we* have the victory! If you believe in the Resurrection Power, then get ready for your resurrection! Death could not hold Him down! Your financial situation *can't* hold you down! Your sickness *can't* hold you down! Your family issues or history *can't* hold you down! Your haters *can't* hold you down! Your storm *can't* hold you down!! Give Him the highest praise because your tomb can't hold you down!

IT'S ALREADY BETTER

James 1:2

For those of you who are going through something right now, this is for you! For those of you who are not going through something, pull this word out of your back pocket when you are going through! It's going to get better! No! It's *already* better!

Life will *always* be filled with trials and tribulations. The Word never mentioned that the road we travel would be easy. How do I know? Jesus is the perfect example that our road will not be easy. If Jesus wasn't exempt from trials and tribulations, what makes you think that you are exempted? We will face adversity! We will face temptation! We will endure some pain! We will cry some tears! We *will* face persecution from others (especially family and friends)! We may experience moments in which it feels that life itself is trying to take us out. We may experience moments in which it feels that we may not see another day! We may see more cloudy days than sunny days! We may feel like giving up and walking away!

But no matter what you are going through, it's going to get better; it's already better! You are probably saying, "How can you say that when you don't know what I am going through?" You're right! I may not know what you are going through, *but* I know *Who* will bring you through!

If you stop and look back over your life, how many times did your situation look dark but get better? How many times when you were down for the count, man counted you out, and God raised you up? I can say it's already better because it is! If you noticed, I didn't say it is going to get better but that it is already better! See, our problem is we speak words that help kill our situation instead of speaking life into our situation, for death and life are in the power of the tongue (let that marinate). It's *already* better!

No matter the weapon attacking your family, your child, your husband, your wife, your marriage, your job, your finances, your health, your peace, your heart, your mind, your spirit, your faith, it will *not* prosper! The dark cloud hanging over you will *not* stay much longer! "Weeping may endure for a night, *but* joy comes in the morning!" All things are working for your good!!

Don't be moved by your circumstances but stand strong knowing your labor is not in vain!! Nobody wants to endure pain, but the pain is necessary to make us stronger! You have endured or may be enduring a lot, but you are *still* here! You can't stop now! You can't stop now because we serve a God who brought us out of storms before! He will bring us out again! We serve a God who will never leave nor forsake us! With God, things will always get better!!

So the next time you feel like walking away, remember it is already better! The next time you look at your bank account, remember it is already better! The next time you feel like giving up, remember it is already better! The next time you are shedding tears in the midnight hour, remember it is already better! The next time you look at your husband or wife, remember it is already better! The next time you look at your child or children, remember it is already better! The next time you get turned down for a promotion, remember it is already better! When you walk through the doors of your job, remember it is already better!

Through the tears and pain, I am encouraging myself that it is already better and want to encourage you that it is already better for you, too! It's already better!

Related Reading

Psalm 30:5b; Isaiah 54:17a; Romans 8:28; 1 Corinthians 15:58

RUN AND TELL IT

Mark 5:14-20

When Jesus went to the country of Gadarenes, He encountered a man who was possessed with a spirit. As soon as the man saw Jesus, he ran to Him and worshiped Him. I would contend that it was the evil spirit in the man that recognized Jesus. The enemy can't help but to acknowledge the presence of Jesus. Luke 4:33-34 says:

> *Now in the synagogue there was a man who had a spirit*
> *of an unclean demon. And he cried out with a loud voice,*
> *saying, 'Let us alone! What have we to do with You, Jesus*
> *of Nazareth? Did You come to destroy us? I know who You*
> *are—the Holy One of God!'*

The enemy will recognize the presence of Jesus before we do (let that marinate). So Jesus called out the spirit in the demon-possessed man and even asked its name. The spirit said that its name was Legion, for it was many. Legion knew the Power that stood before it because it began begging for mercy so to speak. Jesus cast the spirit out of the man into swine that ran violently and ended up drowning in the sea. The man, who was now in his right mind, wanted to stay with Jesus, but Jesus did not permit him to go. Jesus commanded the man to go and tell his friends what took place.

By definition, "testimony" can be defined as a public profession of a religious experience. The formerly demon-possessed man had a testimony, and Jesus wanted him to share it with others. There is power in a testimony. Your testimony tells others about what you have endured! Your testimony tells others how you were able to smile through the storm! Your testimony tells others how you were able to dance in the rain! Your testimony tells others that if God did it for you, He will do it for them, too! You can be a blessing to someone by telling them how you were blessed in your weakest moment! You can be an inspiration to someone by telling them your story which may just be his or her story, too! God can use you to give someone strength to keep pressing just by hearing your testimony!

Being ashamed to tell your testimony is saying that you are ashamed of what God has done for you or that you lack appreciation for what He has done for you (really let that marinate). You never know who needs to hear your testimony! You never know who will be blessed by your testimony! You never know the blessing *you* could receive by sharing your testimony! Don't keep your testimony to yourself. Run and tell it!!!

FIGHT ON!

2 Chronicles 20:15-17

"Fight on" has been in my spirit as a means to encourage me to keep pressing, keep going, and never give up in the midst of my fight. If I am in a fight, then others may be in a fight, too. My fight may not be your fight. Your fight may not be my fight. But we are all in the ring! It is very easy to get discouraged in the fight when it appears that we are losing it! It is very easy to give up the fight when it appears that it has gotten the best of us! It is very easy to walk away from the fight when we don't have any swing left in us!

We have to remember that this will not be the only fight we will face in this thing called life. As a matter of fact, we should remember the fights we faced that He won *for us!* Yes, He won our fights! When David faced Goliath, it was not the stone that brought the giant down but David's faith in God. Because you stayed in the past fights, you won because of your faith. It wasn't your will nor might but your faith!

You may say, "My faith was not that strong," but, well, all it takes is *a little faith.* Matthew 17:20 says:

> *So Jesus said to them, 'Because of your unbelief; for as-*
> *suredly, I say to you, if you have faith as a mustard see, you*
> *will say to this mountain, "Move from here to there," and it*
> *will move; and nothing will be impossible for you.'*

Your faith will activate the power within you to stand strong in your fight. If you have a little faith, God can use it! Ephesians 3:20 says, "Now to Him who is able to do exceedingly abundantly above all that we ask or think, according to the power that works in us." If you have a little, He will exceed it (let that marinate).

My brothers and sisters, don't give up the fight! You have come too far to *only* come this far! You have come too far to turn back! God has brought you this far, so you have to trust that He will continue to take you. "Though He slay me, yet will I trust in Him" (Job 13:15). "Weeping may endure for a night, but *joy* comes in the morning" (Pslam 30:15). We wrestle not against flesh and blood but against principalities, against powers, against the rulers of the darkness of this age, against spiritual hosts of wickedness in the heavenly places. Therefore, put on the *whole* armor of God and fight on (Ephesians 6:12-13).

Don't abort the fight and miss your blessing! Don't throw in the towel because you feel weak but call on God for strength to stay in the fight! Be strong for God is with you, so don't you dare give up! He is walking by your side! God is with us in our fight! You are in the fight, but the battle is God's (let that marinate)! Again, I say, *don't you dare give up!* Fight on! It is not over until God says it is over!

God is able to do what He says He is going to do, so if He says the battle is His, then you keep fighting because He will give you the victory! Stop feeling sorry for yourself! End your pity party! Soak up those crocodile tears; dry your eyes! Keep pushing! Fight through the pain! Fight through your sorrow! Be strong! Stand on His word! "Trust in the Lord with all your heart and lean not on your own understanding" (Proverbs 3:5).

Keep fighting, my brother! Keep fighting, my sister! You are *more* than a conqueror! You *can* do all things through Christ who strengthens you (Phillippians 4:13). Don't give up the fight! Fight on!

DON'T GIVE UP: GOD IS IN CONTROL

In the last few days, the Holy Spirit has spoken words of encouragement from "push through your pain" to "don't throw in the towel!" As I was sitting at my desk, the Holy Spirit said, "The reason why you should keep pushing through your pain instead of throwing in the towel is because *God is in control*, so don't give up!"

The enemy cannot do any more to you than God allows him to do. Let me say that again! The enemy *cannot* do any more to you than God allows him to do. How do I know? It is in the Word!

> *And the Lord said to Satan, "Behold, all that he has is in your power; only do not lay hand on his person." So Satan went out from the presence of the Lord (Job 1:12)*

See, God allowed or permitted Satan to test Job with limitations. God had confidence that, despite what Satan threw at Job, Job would not turn away from Him. Oh, and don't forget that Satan was *not* allowed to take Job out (remember: you shall *live* and not die! Your storm will *not* take you out! Someone needed that!).

God is in control of *all* things, including Satan.

> *"Behold, I have created the blacksmith who blows the coals in the fire, who brings forth an instrument for his work; And I have created the spoiler to destroy. No weapon formed against you shall prosper, And every tongue which rises against you in judgment You shall condemn. This is the heritage of the servants of the Lord, And their righteousness is from Me," says the Lord (Isaiah 54:16-17).*

God created Satan, and since He is the Creator, Satan's power or ability to do things is limited. Any weapon he creates to stop God's purpose will never succeed. You are going through the fire because God trusts you! See, I believe that God allows us to go through things because He trusts we will remain faithful through the storm. Oh, you don't have to believe *me;* it's in the Word.

> *Then the Lord said to Satan, "Have you considered My servant Job, that there is none like him on the earth, a blameless and upright man, one who fears God and shuns evil? And still he holds fast to his integrity, although you incited Me against him, to destroy him without cause" (Job 2:3).*

Whatever you are going through and whenever you go through it, take on the same attitude of Job when he said, "Though He slay me, yet will I trust in Him" (Job 13:15). Though I am dealing with sickness, yet I will trust in Him! Though my body is racking with pain, yet I will trust in Him! Though a loved one is lashing out against me, yet I will trust in Him! Though I don't have any money in my pocket or bank account, yet I will trust in Him! Though I am being mistreated, yet I will trust in Him! Though my friends turned their backs on me, yet I will trust in Him! Though my spouse is not acting right, yet I will trust in Him! Though I am not appreciated at work, yet I will trust in Him! No matter what may come my way, yet I will trust in Him!

Job's story doesn't end with his tribulations but with triumph! Satan's act toward Job did not succeed. As hard as it was, Job remained faithful to God. As hard it may be for you or me, remain faithful to God! Even when his so-called "friends" gave him bad advice (let that marinate), Job remained faithful to God! Job was blessed for his faithfulness. For his faithfulness, God restored all Job had lost plus some! Let me speak this into the atmosphere! For *our* faithfulness, God will restore you and me!

So, as you endure your storm, as you endure the attacks from the enemy, remember that the enemy cannot do any more than God allows! Stand on God's Word, for if He trusted and restored Job, He will do the same for you and me! Keep praying, be steadfast, immovable, and continue to stand on God's Word because He has you, and there is *nothing* Satan can do about it. God is in control!!

DON'T THROW IN YOUR TOWEL

2 Chronicles 15:7

For those of you who may be going through something right now, this is for you! Even if you are not going through something right now, retain this for when you are going through your season! Don't throw in your towel! When a boxer is losing the fight, the coach may think he can't go any further and will have him throw in the towel as a sign of surrender. The boxer may be thinking he has the energy to bounce back and win but will never know because the lack of faith from the coach—which resulted in surrender—was based on what it looked like to *him* from the outside of the ring. Let me throw in this quick nugget. Don't let others convince you to give up the fight all because they think you can't win or that the fight is over (let that marinate).

Oftentimes, we get beat down in our fight and throw in the towel! We get so tired of the stress, heartache, and pain, and we throw in our towel! Instead of enduring the fight, we want to leave the fight. In 2 Chronicles 20:15, we are reminded that the fight is not ours but the Lord's. More specifically, 2 Chronicles 20:17 says, "'You will not *need* to fight in this *battle*. Position yourselves, stand still and see the salvation of the Lord, who is with you, O Judah and Jerusalem!' Do not fear or be dismayed; tomorrow go out against them, for the Lord is with you." If God did not trust you *with* the fight, then He would not allow you to be *in* the fight (let that marinate). Only trained and qualified soldiers are called upon to go to war. You are qualified for your fight, so don't you throw in your towel!

David brought down a man who was bigger than him because he had faith in God who is bigger than all things! David didn't throw in his towel or, more correctly, his slingshot! As a matter of fact, he threw God into it when he spoke to Goliath by saying, "'You come to me with a sword, with a spear, and with a javelin but I come to you in the name of the Lord of hosts, the God of the armies, who you have defied. This day the Lord will deliver you into my hand, and I will strike you and take your head from you'" (1 Sam. 17:45-46a). When you throw in the towel, it is an indication that you have lost faith in your *own* abilities and didn't activate your faith in God to handle it for you (yes, I said it).

Don't throw in your towel because you may be a step away from your breakthrough! Don't throw in your towel because you may be a step away from being delivered from your situation! Don't throw in your towel because you may be moments away from receiving your healing! Don't throw in your towel because you may be on the verge of your victory!

You are a child of the Most High! You are a child of a King! You are *anointed!* You are *more than a conqueror!* You may be weak, but God is your strength!! You may not be able, but God is *more* than able! God is able to do just what He said He will do! He will fulfill *everything* He promised to you! Don't throw in your towel and give up on God because He won't give up on you! He will throw the towel back to you before ever even *thinking* of giving up on you (let that marinate)!

Put down your towel and call upon the name of the Lord who is strong and mighty! "The Lord is mighty in battle! Lift up your heads, O you gates! Lift up, you everlasting doors! And the King of glory shall come in. Who is this King of glory? The Lord of hosts—He is the King of glory" (Ps. 24:8-10)

Victory is on the way! Declare it! As a matter of fact, go ahead and put a praise on it! Praise Him for your breakthrough! Praise Him for your deliverance! Praise Him for your miracle! Praise Him for your healing! Praise Him for your strength! Put a praise on it!

Yes, I just inserted a praise moment because when you think about the goodness of Jesus and all He has done for you, you can't help but praise Him, and I'm putting a praise on your storm because I know He is going to work it out for you! If He works it out for you, then I know He will work it out for me! Only the humble can praise God for blessing someone else while they are waiting on their own blessing (really let that marinate)!

He has brought you this far, so He will continue to carry you. If He brought you to it, He will bring you through it! Don't throw in your towel!

Related Reading

Galatians 6:9; Philippians 4:13

YOU CAN HANDLE IT!

Job 1:8-12

In the midst of my storm and wanting to give up, I questioned God about my storm. I asked God, "God, why would you allow me to go through what I am going through?" He said, "Because you can handle it!" I said, "God, really? Do you not see me now?" He said, "Yes, and I see you after the storm. I knew you would be where you are now, but I also know the outcome. I am the Author of your life, so I *know* your story. My son, you can and *will* handle this!"

My brothers and my sisters, I may not know the full extent of your circumstances, your situation, or your storm, but God wants you to know that you can handle it! As His Word says, He knew you before you were formed in your mother's womb (Jer. 1:5). As a matter of fact, He knew you before your mother and father decided to hook up! He knows every step that we will take in life. God allows us to use free will to decide the way we go, but even if we go the wrong way, He has written a way out! Since He knows everything about us, then we should be still and let God be God!

When God questioned Satan about Job, He had complete faith that Job would not turn away from Him. God "allowed" Satan to cause limited harm to Job. I say limited harm because Satan could not kill Job. This should give you a new perspective on the Scripture, "No weapon formed against you shall prosper" (Is. 54:17). The weapon attacking you has limited power and needs God's permission to attack you (let that marinate)!

Job withstood Satan's attack. I love the statement Job made to God, "'I know that You can do everything, and that no purpose of Yours can be withheld from You'" (Job 42:2). Job was blessed with more in the end than he had before Satan attacked him. I believe that if we are steadfast and immovable, God will bless us with more after the storm than we had *before* the storm because we remained faithful *through* the storm!

With all of that being said, I got this! You got this! We got this! Keep pushing! Keep pressing! Don't give up! Don't give in! Be encouraged! You *can* handle it!

Related Reading

Psalm 46:10a; Jeremiah 1:5a

YOUR BLESSING IS A STEP AWAY

John 5:1-9

If you notice in this account, the sick man's response to Jesus was that there was no one to put him into the pool. I don't proclaim to be an expert on God's Word, and as I read the Scripture, I found it odd that we truly do not know how the sick man got to the pool, a step away from being healed. We do know, however, that he was very close to his deliverance, his breakthrough. Did he get there by operating on his faith or giving up short of his blessing? Oftentimes, when we are a step away from our blessing, we stop doing whatever it was we were doing to get to that point and we start making excuses as to why we can't make that final step (let that marinate).

The sick man said that he didn't have anyone to put him in the pool. Can I help you with something? You can't put your trust in man. Psalm 146:3 says, "Do not put your trust in princes, *nor* in a son of man, in whom there is no help." Our trust should be in God, and when we trust God, He will work through or use man to help us. "Trust in the Lord with all your heart and lean not on your own understanding; In all your ways acknowledge Him, And He shall direct your paths" (Prov. 3:5-6).

The man was sick for 38 years. He was at the pool in his condition for a long time. In my opinion, he made an excuse as to why he hadn't stepped into the pool. He was waiting for someone (man) to put him in the pool. Others were passing him to receive their blessing (how many times have you frowned or "hated" on someone because they were bold enough to get their blessing while you sat there and watched? Let that marinate).

Here is the thing that blew my mind about this account. The sick man never stepped into the pool to be healed. When Jesus showed up (I feel like shouting right there), the sick man was healed! Jesus asked the sick man if he wanted to be made well, and though the sick man did not give a direct "yes," he was *still* healed!

Though the sick man passed blame on others for not receiving the blessing of healing, he was *still* healed! We can only assume that the man had enough faith to get him to the pool, but his faith decreased when he was at the pool. How many of you know that if you have faith the size of a mustard seed, your mountain-sized problems can be moved?! How many of you know that if you have faith the size of a mustard seed, He can do exceedingly abundantly above all you can ask or think according to the power that works in you?! (Eph. 3:20)

Today, be encouraged to keep pressing forward! Today, declare that you will not allow anything or anyone stop you from receiving your blessing! Today, declare that no matter what the situation looks like, your faith will not decrease! Today, declare like Job that "Though they slay me, yet I will trust in Him" (Job 13:15). Today, declare that "*no* weapon formed against me shall prosper" (Is. 54:17). Today, declare that what God has for you is for you and that you *will* receive what He has for you! Today, declare that you will trust God, that you will let God guide your footsteps, and that you *will* step into your blessing! Don't stop! Your blessing is *a step away!*

YOU WILL WIN!

Psalm 108:13 (GNT)

If I may, let me be transparent. I've been in a battle for a long time and feel like I am losing. I've been feeling defeated and, at times, have wanted to raise my white flag in surrender. I asked God, "God, why would you allow me to go through what I am going through?" He said, "Because you can handle it!" I said, "God, really?" Do you not see me now?" He said, "Yes, and I see you after the storm. I knew you would be where you are now but I also know the outcome. I am the Author of your life so I know your story. My son, you *can* and will handle this!" As I thought about the words God spoke to me, the Holy Spirit said, "You *will* win!"

You *will* win! The enemy may be attacking your finances! The enemy may be attacking your family! The enemy may be lurking on your job ready to attack you! The enemy may be attacking your marriage! The enemy may be attacking your character! The enemy may be attacking you from all directions! But I want you to know and even remind myself, we *will* win! God did not bring us this far so we can be defeated! It is time for us to get up and walk in victory! Jesus told the paralytic man in John 5:8, "Rise, take up your bed and walk." We need to take up our beds and walk in victory because we *will* win!

I don't care what your situation looks like! I don't even have to understand your situation! I don't care if you are tired, stressed, worried, busted, or disgusted! I don't care how long you have felt defeated! As a matter of fact, let me take this moment to speak to myself in my battle! Let me prophesy to myself:

I am a *conqueror* and not defeated! I am the *head* and not the tail I am *above* and not beneath! I am the child of a *Champion!*

Now let me speak to you! You are a *conqueror* and not defeated! You are the *head* and not the tail! You are *above* and not beneath! You are the child of a *Champion!* If you believe you will win, open up your mouth and tell your situation "*I will win!*"

Now, you can't say that you will win and also look *defeated!* Take off defeat and put on your victory attire! Take off your "sorry" shoes and put on your combat boots! It's time to put on your Sunday's best, your best cologne/perfume (because defeat stinks), hold your head high, and walk in victory! You are a child of the great and mighty God! You are anointed! Don't fold under pressure and don't give in to the pressure of your storm! Through the hurt, tears, and pain, keep fighting! You are a *winner!* You *will* win!!

Related Reading

1 Corinthians 15:57; Philippians 4:13

GOD WILL MAKE A WAY

Exodus 14:13-14, 26-31

The Holy Spirit reminded me about a thought given to me over a year ago. This is a reminder for some and good news for others! I don't know what you are going through, and you don't have a clue what I am going through. But what I *do* know is Who will bring us through! Our situation looks as if there is no way out, but God has already worked it out for us to come out! We have to keep believing in Him and hearing His voice to come out!

There is no way out when we follow our *own* ways, but there will *always* be a way when we follow *God's* ways! I can imagine that many of you reading this are saying, "You don't know the size of the mountain in my way." Maybe you are thinking, "It is easy for you to say what you are saying because you are not me and not going through what I am going through." News flash! You are *not* the only one who has some mountains in this life! You are *not* the only one going through something! You are not the only one battling some "giants!"

Don't look at a person and assume that he or she has it all together (let that marinate). God's grace and mercy cover others so they don't look like what they have been through or are going through! God's grace and mercy help them from throwing a pity party so others won't see what they are going through (let that marinate). We are *all* going through something. If you are not going through something now, brace yourself because it is on the way! But have no fear! God will make a way!

God will move the mountain that is hindering your progress! God will bring down the walls that are hindering you from receiving your blessings! God will bring down the "giants" that are standing in the way of your blessings! God will go before you and make your crooked path straight! But you have to let God have His way in order for Him to make a way! You *have* to be still and let God take the lead!

Exodus 14:14 says, "The Lord will fight for you, and you shall hold your peace." If you let God make a way, He will give you a peace that surpasses all understanding (Phil. 4:7). If you let God make a way, He will give you peace that will sustain you in the storm! If you let God make a way, He *will* make a way!

Hold on, my brothers; hold on, my sisters! Don't give up and don't give in! Despite what I am going through, I *refuse* to give up! I *refuse* to give in! The weight of my storm may put me on my knees, but it will put me in the right position to call on the strength of the Lord. Therefore, I *will* rise! God will not bring you this far and leave you. As a matter of fact, He will *never* leave nor forsake you! You are still here because He made a way for you to be here.

If He made a way before, then He *will* make a way again and again and again!

GOD'S PLAN: PROSPERITY, PROTECTION, HOPE, A FUTURE

Jeremiah 29:11-14

God has a plan for your life despite what may be going on in it right now. Just like a good chess master, God strategically places us or uses our wrong moves for His will! Don't think because you are in a corner that the game is over; it's just the beginning! The Word says that His plan is for us to prosper (Jer. 29:11), which is not limited to finances (let that marinate)! The Word says that His plan comes with insurance, which is His protection!

"The name of the Lord is a strong tower; the righteous run to it and are safe" (Prov. 18:10). "Yea, though I walk through the valley of the shadow of death, I will fear no evil; for You are with me, Your rod and Your staff, they comfort me" (Psa. 23:4). The Word says His plan gives us hope, so there is no need to doubt in your situations, no need to question, no need to fear. Instead, let your soul rest because He provides hope! The Word says that His plan is for us to have a future, so your situation is not dead but about to be resurrected! Your "bones" will live according to Ezekiel 37:1-10 (let that marinate)! I see you in the future, and you look much better than you do right now!

Since you know He has some plans for you, call on Him! Seek Him with your whole heart! Pray and He *will* listen to you! The devil couldn't kill you because God had His hands on you and His angels encamped around you! You were able to bounce back after being deflated in your situation because God breathed life back into you; He restored you! God will bring you back from depression! God will bring you back from addiction! God will bring you back from brokenness! God will bring your health back! God will bring your marriage back! God will bring you back from your situation, your circumstances, your storm because He has plans for you!

MAKE IT TREMBLE

James 2:19

In the Scripture, the demons believed in God and trembled in fear of God. The demon possessing the man cried out to Jesus and asked Jesus to leave him alone. Jesus rebuked the demon, and the demon came out of the man. Even the demons recognized Jesus as the Holy One. Though they may have been disobedient *to* Jesus, they knew the power *of* Jesus! Could it be that the demons in your situation are not afraid to leave because you haven't invited Jesus to step into it? Could it be you are constantly in darkness because you haven't ushered in the light of Jesus to shine in your situation?

Now watch this! When the exorcists attempted to call out the spirits, those spirits acknowledged that they knew Jesus, they knew Paul, but they didn't know the men trying to cast them out. Since they were not afraid of the men, they overpowered and wounded the men. Could it be that darkness continues to overpower you because you are relying on the prayers of your pastor, big momma, or friends rather than your own prayers? Could it be that your situation is wounding you because the God in you cannot be seen?

We spend more time talking *about* our situation instead of speaking to our situation! We will complain about how big our problem is instead of praising our big God! When I started speaking to my situation instead of about my situation, I noticed a change! When I stopped talking about believing in God and allowed my beliefs to show through my actions, I noticed a change! When I put my faith glasses back on and took off my natural eyes (we walk by faith and not by sight), I noticed a change (2 Cor. 5:7). When my words, my heart, and my spirit aligned with the Word, I noticed a change! When I took me out of it and put Jesus into it, I noticed a change!

How many of you want to notice a change? How many of you want to experience a change? The change begins with you! You have the power to change, and all you have to do is call on the main source of Power to drive the spirits out! At the mention of the name of Jesus, demons tremble! Speak Jesus in your house and watch the demons tremble! Speak Jesus on your job and watch the demons tremble! Speak Jesus over yourself and watch the demons tremble! But don't forget, if you don't truly know Jesus and only speak *about* the Jesus spoken to you through your pastor, your big momma, or your friends, the demons won't move (let that marinate).

I declare, I decree, and I believe that we can make our situations tremble by bringing Jesus into them! I don't know about you, but I'm ready for the demons to depart from me and those connected to me. I would contend that, as children of God, we will always be under demonic attack, but we have a Savior ready to step in to save us from them. Jesus is the Savior! I don't know what your situation may be at this present time, but I believe if we (you and I) call on the name of Jesus, we can make it tremble. The darkness will flee, and you will see the light!

Make it Tremble!

Related Reading

Mark 1:23-26; Acts 19:13-16

HOLD ON TO THE STRUGGLE

Genesis 32:24-29

If you are familiar with this account and Jacob, then you may recall that Jacob had some struggles in life. He struggled with his brother Esau. He struggled with Labon. Later in life, one could contend that he was indirectly connected to the struggle between Joseph and his brothers—Jacob's sons. The primary fact was Jacob had some struggles. If Jacob had some struggles, then we should be reminded that we will have some struggles as well.

Blessed people are not exempt from struggles (let that marinate). In the account, Jacob wrestled with a "Man" whom is believed to be an angel of God. When the "Man" said, "Let Me go, for the day breaks," Jacob said he would not let Him go until He blessed him! Jacob did not let go! Because Jacob struggled with God and men but prevailed (won), he was blessed! Just think, if Jacob had let go of the "Man" when He asked to be let go, he (Jacob) would have let go of his blessing, too (let that marinate).

My brothers and sisters, there is nothing easy or pretty about the struggles we endure in life. The tenacity of Jacob as he held on to the "Man" resulted in a blessing! Do you have the same tenacity to hold on during your struggle (really let that marinate)? Let's be honest or, better yet, let me be honest. There are times I've thought it would be easier to simply let go of the struggle versus holding on during the struggle. However, the Spirit in me will not allow the man in me to let go during the struggle due to the blessing that will come after the struggle.

The struggle is real, but the blessing after the struggle is real, too! Jacob held on to the "Man" until the morning and was blessed! My brothers and sisters, hold on! "Weeping may endure for a night, but *joy* comes in the morning (Ps. 30:5). Your struggle may endure for a night, but your blessing will come in the morning! Get a real good grip and hold on! Hold on to God's unchanging hand, and He will sustain you in the midst of your struggle! You can hold on! I can hold on! I *will* hold on! You will prevail over your struggle! I will prevail over my struggle! Together, we will be *blessed* after the struggle!

Hold on to the struggle! It will bless you!

MY WILL BE DONE

Matthew 6:10

Recently, I asked God why He would allow me to endure my current storm. He said, "My will be done." Naturally, my response was, "What do You mean 'My will be done'? How can hurt be part of Your will? How can pain be part of Your will? How can I count it all joy when I am not feeling any joy?" He said, "My will be done." Again, my response was, "What do You mean 'My will be done'? I don't understand. I know I heard Your voice loud and clear and believed what You said. However, I've ended up here broken, and You're telling me Your will be done? He said, "Yes, My will be done. I see you, I hear you, and I believe in you, so you believe in Me. This time was written before you were born as part of My will, and I know the outcome. Therefore, lean not on your own understanding and, instead, trust Me!"

When you are going through a storm, it is hard to imagine that God would allow you to endure a broken heart. When you are going through a storm, it is hard to imagine that God would allow you to endure sickness. When you are going through a storm, it is hard to imagine that God would permit bad things to happen to you. Believe it or not, it is part of His plan. It was part of His plan to allow Job to endure the attacks of Satan, and we know how that account ended! It was part of His plan to let Lazarus die and be raised up days later! It was part of

71

His plan for His Son to give His life at Calvary and rise three days later!

His will is *intentional!* All things work for our good! The hurt and pain work for our good! The sleepless nights work for our good! The tears work for our good! He knows the plans that He has for you and me, and I don't believe that His plans include failure! His plans do not include defeat! We may not be able to see how He is intentional, but we have to trust Him!

We didn't see it before, yet He made a way. He will make a way again! We didn't know if we were going to make it through the storm, but He made a way! We didn't know if we were going to pass the test resulting in our testimony, but He made a way! We didn't know if we were going to win the battle, but He made a way! When it looked like it was over, He made a way! He made a way because your assignment in His will is not complete yet! He made a way because of His will!

My brothers and sisters, your days may be cloudy, but the sun *will* shine! You may be hurting, but joy is on the way! You are *still* standing! You are *still* here! It is not by your might but by His will! His will *shall* be done!

Related Reading

Jeremiah 29:11-13 (NIV); Romans 8:28

I'M POSSIBLE WILL MAKE A WAY

Matthew 19:26

"In the beginning, God created the heavens and the earth (Gen. 1:1). He spoke light into existence. His words separated the waters from dry land. Through His words, He made two distinct lights, sun and moon, and created the stars. He spoke life to the birds of the air and creatures of the sea, beasts of the earth. All of these things and more were created as a result of God speaking life to them.

Oftentimes, we encounter situations or circumstances that convince us to believe there is no way out. We encounter or create problems that seem to have no resolution. We become distraught or stressed to a point that hinders our ability to function effectively at home, work, school, church, etc. The consumption of our issue(s) hinders our thinking, clouds our vision, and decreases our faith. The struggle of our situation, circumstance, or storm drains us mentally, physically, and spiritually. We look at our situation, circumstance, or storm and give it power by speaking "the impossible."

Proverbs 18:21 says, "Death and life are in the power of the tongue, and those who love it will eat its fruit." Our situations and circumstances embrace and feed off the words we speak or thoughts we think. They grow stronger and hold us hostage because we give them dominion and authority over us instead of activating our dominion and authority to weaken them and be freed from them!

Don't allow your situation, your circumstances, your storm to convince you that it is impossible for you to win! Don't allow your situation, your circumstances, your storm to convince you that it is impossible for things to change in your favor! As a matter of fact, turn around and thank your situation, your circumstances, your storm for putting you in the impossible position! Tell your situation, your circumstance, your storm "thank you" for placing you in the right position! Tell your situation, your circumstance, your storm that you *will* think the impossible! Yes, I said it! Tell it you *will* think the impossible!

Jesus said, "With men this is impossible, but with God all things are possible" (Matt. 19:36). Here is the revelation I received from the words spoken by Jesus. When you speak the impossible in faith, you are acknowledging that the impossible is possible with God. It's a play on words. With your worldly eyes, you see "impossible." But with your spiritual eyes, you should see "I'm Possible."

If God created the heavens and the earth out of nothing, then He can turn your nothing into something! If God can speak light into existence, then He can shine His light on your situation and guide you out of it! If God can move mountains, then He can surely move your mole hill problem! If God can part the Red Sea and make a way out of no way for the children of Israel, then He can part your situation and make a way out of no way! By speaking "I'm Possible," you can take back the dominion and authority you gave to your situation, your circumstance, or your storm and kill it! By speaking "I'm Possible," you are telling your situation, your circumstance, or your storm that *you* will live and *it* will die!

When you are faced with an impossible situation, rejoice and give thanks! When your back is against the wall and things appear to be impossible, rejoice and give thanks! The impossible only confirms the "I'm Possible" God is present and in control! "I'm Possible" *will* make a way! He did it before, and He will surely do it again!

Related Reading

Genesis 18:14a; Jeremiah 32:17; Luke 1:37

THE LORD WILL FIGHT FOR YOU

2 Chronicles 20:15-17

Perhaps, one of the most memorable lines from the movie *The Color Purple* came from the character Sophia, "All my life I had to fight." I think some of us can relate to Ms. Sophia, as we have had to fight for whatever reason (family, spouse, work, finances, health, etc.), during our lifetime thus far. Fighting requires you to exert a lot of energy. If it continues for a long period of time, fighting can wear you down until you can fight no more. Fighting is a struggle in the sense that one thing is trying to overpower the other, and if both parties are equally strong, there is no telling when the fight will end. Fighting can take a physical, mental, and spiritual toll on you. If you feel as if you are losing, it can discourage you from continuing the fight, which may lead in either defeat or surrender.

At some point in the fight, we have to realize that our worldly efforts are a moot point in a spiritual battle, for the Word says in Ephesians 6:12, "For we do not wrestle against flesh and blood, but against principalities, against powers, against the rulers of the darkness of this age, against spiritual hosts of wickedness in the heavenly places." At some point in the fight, we have to realize that the fight is bigger than us and requires intervention from our Mighty God.

We are quick to quote a portion of 2 Chronicles 20:15, "The battle is not yours, but God's," but we don't truly give it to God. The battle is not ours but God's! The fight is not ours but God's! The struggle is not ours but God's! You don't have to fight any more! This is not to say you are giving up, so don't feel that way. You are merely moving yourself out of the way so God can have His way! Psalm 46:10a says, "Be still, and know that I am God" which reminds us to surrender our ways and trust God! All we have to do is show up to the fight, stay in the fight, and God will fight for us! It's hard to win a fight if you don't show up to the fight (let that marinate)!

You have been fighting all your life. Now it is time to give the fight to God! I know He will! He said He will! He *will* fight my battles! He *will* fight your battles! If I will be still, He will fight for me! If you will be still, He will fight for you! The Lord *will* fight for you!

Related Reading

Exodus 14:13-14

IN THE FIRE, STAY IN IT

Malachi 3:2-3

If you think about the summer months, the first thing that may come to mind is the hot temperatures you endure depending upon your location. Many of us cannot stand the heat and seek shelter to keep us cool. Though natural heat can be detrimental to our health, spiritual heat is necessary to grow closer to Him. What do you mean? The messenger of God's Word said, "For He is like a refiner's fire and like launderers soap" (Malachi 3:2).

If you are familiar with a refinery, then you know that the purpose of the factory is to transform a raw product into a useful product. For example, we spend billions in off-shore drilling to extract crude oil from the earth. The oil is collected, shipped to various refineries, and transformed into hundreds of products such as the oil in your car. In order to get to the end product, extreme heat is used to separate the bad stuff, the crud, the crap, the unnecessary things from the good things resulting in the desired product (let that marinate).

Once the separation is complete, the product goes through a few cleaning stages until the end result has been achieved. The process is necessary for the desired result! The fire is necessary to refine you! The fire is necessary to purify you! The fire is necessary to separate some stuff from you! The fire is necessary to separate some people from you! The refining process you endure is necessary for His will!

How many times have you felt like you were in a fire and wanted to get out? Have you ever wondered that maybe, just maybe, it was necessary for you to stay in the fire so you could be purified? When things get hot, we want to get out of the kitchen (I know I am not by myself). But when I read the Scripture, it revealed that, instead of asking to be removed from the fire, maybe I should seek God to comfort me during the fire. Shadrach, Meshach and Abed-Nego did not try to leave the fiery furnace but were at peace in the furnace. See, when the furnace was opened, three men went in, but their enemies saw a fourth appear who was like the Son of God! Even in the fire, Peace is with you (let that marinate)!

Just like storms, there are three stages of fire:

1. You are going into a fire.

2. You are standing in the midst of a fire.

3. You are coming out of a fire.

If we don't endure the fire, we may miss out on a blessing. Everyone has some stuff that needs to be removed from them spiritually. I know I have some stuff that needs to be removed from me spiritually, which is encouragement to stay in the fire despite how hot it may get in the fire! Despite my fire, I know God is with me! Despite your fire, God is with you, too! He said that He would never leave nor forsake us, so even in the fire, He is with us!

The next time you feel like you have been placed in the frying pan at work, at home, wherever, seek God to give you the strength and comfort to endure the extreme heat and know that He is with you in the fire. Let Him have His way with you and remove that which is no longer needed. You will come out as *pure gold!!*

YOU ARE A BLESSING: WALK LIKE IT

Joshua 1:3-5

God told Joshua that He was giving him the land; every place he walked would be given to him! From what I know about Joshua, he didn't walk in God's promise with his head held down. He walked into the promise with his head held high like a conqueror. He walked into the promise with a victorious mindset and not a victim spirit! See, real fighters don't fight or walk with their heads down but hold their heads up ready to fight!

Even when we are winning the battle, we will hold our heads down because our eyes deceive us into thinking we are losing (ooh wee, please let that marinate). God told Joshua what to do to claim the blessing, and Joshua followed the instructions to receive the blessing. He didn't walk from it but walked to it! Joshua didn't cower in fear in battle but fought courageously in battle! Just like God promised, no man was able to stand against Joshua, and He was always with him!

What does this have to do with you? It is time that you truly embrace that you are a child of God, God's *blessing*, and you should walk like it! It is time that I truly embrace that I am a child of God, His *blessing*, and I should walk like it! It's neither boastfulness nor conceit but recognition of who we are *and* Whose we are! I can personally attest to the fact that, at times, I have walked around with a defeated mindset and even have had setbacks once in a while. Yes, the minister is not super spiritual and has his own kryptonite (aka weakness).

When it appeared things may not work in my favor, down went my head (not literally but spiritually). When promotions didn't come through, down went my head. When some turned their backs on me, down went my head. But then, the lightbulb came on, and I began to see who I was! I recognized, embraced, and surrendered to my purpose. I realized that God had me where He wanted me to be and would continue to take me where He wanted to take me for His will. I realized that God created the blessing of me to be a blessing and that blessings would come as a result of blessing others (let that marinate).

I began to speak to myself, "I am a blessing; I am *anointed.*" The Holy Spirit began to show me the blessings of me! When people couldn't understand how I was able to do the job of 6 to 7 people, the Spirit said, "It's because you are a blessing!" When some couldn't understand how things that use to stress me don't bother me anymore, the Spirit said, "It's because you are a blessing!" When people wondered why I walked away from an area and they were no longer successful, the Spirit said, "It's because you are a blessing!" Even now, when I am going through something and question why I am going through it, the Spirit says, "It's because you are a blessing!"

You are a blessing, so walk like it! Because you are a blessing, everywhere you go will be blessed! Your place of work will be blessed! Your home *will* be blessed! Your community *will* be blessed! Everywhere you go *will* be blessed! Everywhere you step *will* be blessed! If people don't appreciate the blessing of you, don't lose any sleep over it because I promise you that they will miss the blessing when it leaves.

Like an umbrella in the rain, the blessing of you covers everyone connected to you. So, when the blessing moves and they don't move with you, they are not covered by the blessing (let that marinate). These are not mere words but part of my testimony! Oh, some people may think they can hold down, hold back, or even stop the blessing of you. But they forget that He sets a table for us before our enemies and that He makes our enemies our footstool. The ones who try to hinder the blessing of you will be used to raise up the blessing for all to see!

Our life journey is not easy. God never promised an easy journey, but He did promise to be with us always! Through the storms, the sunshine, and the rain, God is with us! If God is with us, then who can be against us? Don't walk in fear or a defeated mindset; walk like a conqueror! You are a *blessing*, so walk like it!

Related Reading

Romans 8:31; 2 Timothy 1:7

YOU ARE CHOSEN

1 Peter 2:9-10

The purpose of this thought is to remind you that you were chosen with a purpose! God did not create you to just exist but created you with a purpose. Life has a way of making you think that you are a mistake. You are *not* a mistake! The devil will try to tell you that God doesn't have a plan for your life, but the devil is a lie! God has the power to take your mess and turn it into a blessing, not only for you but for others.

As God's chosen, your purpose will be revealed at the appointed time. When your purpose is revealed, it will be revealed among the people. God will prepare you privately so your purpose can be revealed publicly! So don't rush it, but let God have His way!

Don't think that you are not ready to operate in your purpose. You *are* ready! How do I know? If you look back over your life, the things you have gone through have merely been a preparation period for your purpose. You can't put a pot roast in a microwave and expect good results. It may be semi-raw, undercooked, and make you sick when consumed. But if you put the pot roast in the oven at the right temperature, for the right amount of time (slow roast), it will be well-seasoned, moist, just right to eat.

The preparation period allows God to equip you for your purpose. I can personally look back over my life and say that who I was spiritually in June 2009 is not the same person who delivered his first sermon on July 30, 2014. God used that time prior to the public revealing of my purpose to equip me for my purpose (let that marinate). You are ready!

If you embrace the fact that you are chosen with a purpose, you are *ready* for your purpose, and you are equipped for your purpose, then you must show no fear and *commit* to your purpose. After it was announced that Solomon would be king, David told Solomon to know God and serve Him with a loyal heart and willing mind. David was speaking about his commitment! As God's chosen, you have to be committed to Him. The fact we are His chosen tells us that He is committed to us, so we should be committed to Him. You can't turn on your commitment at your convenience but must keep it on continuously for His will! With your commitment, do not be afraid of your purpose! He chose you for a purpose and will be with you until your purpose has been fulfilled!

So today and every day, speak this over yourself:

"I am chosen! I am *chosen* for this generation! I am a member of the chosen generation, the royal priesthood, the holy nation, His own special people. I proclaim the praises of Him who called me out of darkness into His marvelous light. I am His willing vessel! I am committed! I am not alone, for He is with me! I will be His example! I will be the one! I will do what He calls me to do! Because He chose me, I will trust Him! In the name of Jesus, I am *chosen!*"

You are *chosen!!*

Related Reading

1 Chronicles 28:5-6

YOU ARE QUALIFIED

1 Samuel 17:31-37

One day, I was reading the account of David and Goliath from the perspective of: speak to bring your "giant" down. After I completed the thought, I was guided back to what took place before Goliath was defeated. David left his duties of watching the flock to join the army in battle with the Philistines. If you notice, David was ready to fight, but Saul tried to disqualify him by saying that he was not able to fight because he was a youth and Goliath was a man.

Now, keep in mind that Saul was the king, and they (he and David) were on the same side or team. It is amazing how the ones who may try to disqualify you from doing something are the people who are in your corner (really let that marinate). I like to believe that they try to disqualify you from doing something because they have disqualified themselves from doing the very thing that you are courageous enough to do (help me, Holy Spirit. Let that marinate, too).

Here is the good news! Man cannot disqualify what God has already qualified. David's response to Saul explained why he was qualified to fight the Philistine. Man will try to disqualify you for not knowing the prerequisites you have completed that qualify you to do what God wants you to do. Don't forget, Saul was the current king, and David was the future, anointed king (read 1 Samuel 16:1-13). The future king brought down the "giant" of the current king; word to you, you may be qualified to take down the generational "giants" of those before you so those after you will not have to face them!

Again, man cannot disqualify what God has already qualified. You don't have to argue, defend, or debate someone when they say you are not qualified. They don't know the pre-work or basic training you have completed that qualifies you for your assignment. "Now to Him who is able to do exceedingly abundantly above all that we ask or think, according to the power that works in us" (Eph 3:20). You are able because He is able, and because *He* is able, you are qualified!!

YOU ARE MORE THAN A CONQUEROR

Romans 8:37

Simply put, you are not just a conqueror but you ARE more than a conqueror! You can and you *will* conquer the very thing that you are in now or whatever God allows you to go through. You can and you *will* conquer the "giant" (i.e. financial debt, depression, generational curses, etc.) that has been standing in your life far too long! Time for the giant to fall!!!

We have to realize that our battles are fixed! We have to see that our battles are rigged! The enemy can't win a battle that has been fixed in your favor! You are more than a conqueror because your love for God enables you to lean on Him even more during your trials and tribulations. And when you lean on Him, you are telling your storm that the battle is not yours but God's, and your storm knows it can't stand against our Almighty God!

You are more than a conqueror, and conquerors do not walk around with a defeated mindset! Your walk should be strong! Your walk should be courageous! Your walk should encourage someone to pick himself up and change his walk! You are more than a conqueror, and conquerors do not walk around with the heads held down but with their heads held high! You are more than a conqueror because you are led by Jesus who *always* triumphs over the enemy! You are more than a conqueror because we have the victory through Jesus! You are more than a conqueror because you are a child of God, and children of God are *overcomers!*

You are not just a conqueror! You are *more than a conqueror!!*

Related Reading

1 Corinthians 15:57; 2 Corinthians 2:14; 1 John 5:4

YOU ARE A WINNER AND AN OVERCOMER

1 John 4:4

My brothers and sisters, you may be going through a storm at this very moment and may feel ready to give up. You have shed your share of tears and probably don't have any more left. The weight of your storm is wearing you down and becoming unbearable. It seems as if the storm will not cease. You have lost your confidence and are allowing your storm to control you. You have been walking around in defeat and are ready to throw in the towel.

My brothers and sisters, I want to remind you that you are a winner and an overcomer! No weapon formed against you shall prosper! You can do *all* things through Christ who strengthens you! Yet in all these things, we are more than conquerors! In spite of your storm! In spite of your circumstances! In spite of whatever you may be going through right now, my brothers and sisters, you are a winner and an overcomer!

Greater is He who is in me than He that is in the world (1 John 4:4). When people see you, they shouldn't see defeat, but they should see victory! They should see someone who knows they are above and not beneath! They should see someone who knows they are the head and not the tail! They should see someone who knows they are not a chump but a winner! They should see a miracle in the making!

You've had your moment. You've had your pity party. You've been walking around with your head down. But today, it's time to move beyond your moment! Today, it is time to end the pity party! Today, it is time for you to hold your head high and look to the Source of your help! Today is the day that you decree that you shall win! Today is the day that you tell yourself "I am a *winner!*" Today is the day that you declare you are an overcomer!

No situation, no storm, no circumstance is too big for our God to handle! There is nothing God cannot move out of our way! He can make a way out of no way. If God can part the Red Sea, then He can part your situation and make a way for you! If David can believe God to bring down Goliath, then you can believe in God to bring down the giant you are facing! If God can shake the foundations of the prison and loosen the chains that bound Paul, then He can cause a shaking in your situation and loosen the chains that have you bound! Here is some more good news! God does not orchestrate the storm, but He *will* orchestrate the victory from the storm because all things work for our good!

God does not create weak soldiers but births champions! There is a champion in you that is ready to rise up so you can win! There is a champion in you that is ready to overcome your storm. Unleash the champion in you! When you unleash the champion in you, you will look like a winner! When you unleash the champion in you, you will look like an overcomer! When you unleash the champion in you, you will win, and you will overcome the storm! If you believe you are winner, say "I am a winner!" If you believe you are an overcomer, say "I am an overcomer!" Don't give up and don't give in! Stay in the fight! I promise if you stay in the fight, you *will* win and you *will* overcome!

You got this! You are a winner and an overcomer!

Related Reading

Psalm 27:1; Isaiah 54:17a; Romans 8:28, 37; Philippians 4:13

PRESS TO YOUR PROMISE

Hebrews 10:35-39

Your labor is not in vain! Your pain is not in vain! Don't give up because of what you are going through but keep pressing so you can get to what awaits you. Turning back is easy because you can walk down an already traveled road. But why would you want to turn back or turn away from your blessing? God never said that the road we travel would be easy.

You have to get it in your spirit that you will have to keep pressing! You have to get it in your spirit that you will seek the Kingdom of God and His righteousness! You have to set your ways to align with His ways, your thoughts to align with His thoughts! You have come too far to go back. Tell yourself, "I won't go back. I can't turn back. I've come too far to turn back now. I'm walking with the Lord."

Even in the midst of the storm, there is peace! If you simply call on the name of Jesus, He can steady your ship, calm the waves, and help you get through. The Lord will do what He said He would do. He says, "Just believe in Me, put your trust in Me, and the words I've spoken will come to pass. My words will not return to me void but will accomplish what I sent them out to accomplish. Don't let the enemy fool you into doing something outside My will. Trust in Me, and I will see you through it and to it! Be of good cheer and encouraged by My words. I've done it before and will do again. Have patience and wait on Me! Hold strong and wait on Me! Just believe it will come to pass!"

Thank God for the promises! Hallelujah! Everything He has told you, believe it! He is sure to come through! Don't give up! Don't give up! Just when you are ready to give up, that's when He will step in, show Himself strong, and prove Himself to you! He *will* come through! Don't turn away but press toward your promise! Your reward awaits and is ready to be received by you. Go and get it!

Father God, thank You for another opportunity to travel the path ordained for our lives. We have made up in our minds that we won't go back to those things that You delivered us from! We have made up in our minds that we will not open doors that have been closed by You! We have made up in our minds that we won't turn back! We will press through our trials! We will press through our mess! We will stand strong in the midst of the battle, for we know it is not ours but Yours. We will press on so You can get the glory! Lord, continue to be with us on this journey. As we lift You up, continue to lift us up. These and other blessings we ask in Your Son Jesus's name. Amen!

ENDURE THE PAIN

1 Chronicle 4:9-10

Jabez was named as such because his mother experienced pain with him. A woman cannot be impregnated today and give birth to a full-term baby tomorrow. It takes time for the embryo to develop or transform into the baby. The birth of the child (blessing) is a process (let that marinate)! During a pregnancy, a mother may experience some type or some level of pain as the baby goes through the developmental stages in the womb. She presses through the pain because of the blessing growing inside of her. She presses forward and endures the pain because she knows a blessing is on the way.

The mother is not comfortable during the pregnancy as she endures changes to her body in support of her baby. You will not be comfortable as you endure changes to prepare you for your blessing! I would think that the greatest pain comes when it is time to deliver the baby. The pain intensifies right before the blessing is birthed. Your pain will intensify right before the birth of your blessing!

When the baby arrives and the pain subsides, the blessing becomes the focus. When the mother looks at her child, she smiles (through the pain) because the blessing of her newborn was worth the process. Mothers endure pain for the blessing of their children! Can you endure the pain for your blessing?

Your blessing is being developed or formed as we speak. You will have to endure some changes to accommodate the delivery of your blessing. Just as a patient is prepped for surgery, God preps us for our blessing (let that marinate). In order for God to bless you, He has to enlarge your boundaries which will come with some pain. The pain represents the preparation necessary to receive the blessings He has for you. It is necessary to endure the pain, as it repairs some stuff, tears down some stuff, removes some stuff, or destroys some stuff we no longer need. After the pain comes healing, restoration, transformation, strength, peace, the blessing! Like the saying goes, "No pain, no gain."

There is one other who endured great pain, and His name is Jesus! Jesus endured the greatest pain of all so we could have the blessing of eternal salvation. Can you imagine how our lives would be if Jesus had not endured His painful purpose? My God! Thank you, Jesus, for enduring the pain for our salvation!

You may be going through something right now! You may be experiencing some pain! Though I don't know the level of pain you are experiencing, I want to encourage you to endure the pain! If I can be transparent, I am experiencing a pain unlike any other (as we speak) that I've experienced before, excruciating pain! But I am pressing forward because I believe God is going to bless me (double for my trouble), and the pain will be worth enduring for my blessing!

No weapon formed against you shall prosper! If you couldn't handle the pain, then God would not let you experience the pain (let that marinate)! If you were not anointed for the pain, then God would not let you experience the pain! If you were not qualified for the pain, then God would not let you experience the pain! Your pain has a purpose! Don't be discouraged by the pain but keep pressing because He will pull you through! You may be experiencing some pain, but know it will result in a blessing!

Related Reading

2 Corinthians 12:7-10

WORK YOUR FAITH

Mark 5:25-34

The woman with the issue of blood suffered with her affliction for twelve years. From the Scripture, we can say that she tried everything earthly possible to find a cure for her affliction and was steadfast in her efforts. She heard about Jesus and went to Him; she didn't wait for Him to come to her (let that marinate). Jesus was in the midst of a crowd. If you've ever been at a concert or a place with a large crowd, then you know how much energy it takes to get through the crowd to a specific destination. The uniqueness of this account is the fact that the woman was in pain, yet she pushed through to get to Jesus!!

Even in the midst of your pain, you still have to P.U.S.H. (Pray Until Something Happens) through to get your breakthrough (let that marinate, too). The woman believed her healing would come from simply touching Jesus. Subconsciously, she could have thought that His glory would flow down. Hence, the hem of His garment would contain enough glory to heal her. Immediately, Jesus felt power leaving when she touched Him. The woman believed that if she touched Jesus, then she would be healed. However, Jesus said it was her faith that made her well. The woman achieved healing by working her faith.

James 2:26 says, "For as the body without the spirit is dead, so faith without works is dead also." If you say you have faith, then work it! Oftentimes, *we* (not the enemy) allow our storms, issues, circumstances, situations, etc. to control our faith. When we should turn on more of our faith, we turn it off. As the current young generation would say, our faith should be "turnt up" and should "turn down" for nothing!

If the woman had not worked her faith, she would not have been healed. We have to work our faith to receive our healing! We have to work our faith to change our situation! We have to work our faith to get our breakthrough! If we would work our faith, our work would be exceeded. How do I know this? Ephesians 3:20 says, "Now to Him who is able to do exceedingly abundantly above all that we ask or think, according to the power that works in us." If we have faith in Him and allow Him to work in us, then He will move in our situation and abundantly exceed our expectations, needs, etc.!

If you don't work your faith, it won't work for you! While you work your faith, keep P.U.S.H.ing. It will work in your favor!

Related Reading

James 2:26

YOU GOTTA WORK FOR IT!

Joshua 6:1-5

It is amazing how one can read the same Scripture repetitively and realize different messages if he or she maintains an open heart, mind, and spirit to receive that Scripture (let that marinate). As Chapter 6 of Joshua begins, God tells Joshua that the city of Jericho will be given to him, and then He proceeds to tell Joshua how it will be given to him. At any time, Joshua could have chosen to do his own thing, but he followed God's command.

When you follow your own will or implement your plan B in place of God's plan A, things do not work out the way they would have if the original plan had been followed (let that marinate). Yes, we believe Romans 8:28, "And we know that all things work together for good to those who love God, to those who are the called according to His purpose," so even if I do my own thing, it will eventually work out. But if I do what He commands me to do, it will work out a lot sooner rather than later without my interference of His plan.

God will give you the promise and tell you what you need to do to receive the promise. God promised the victory of Jericho and provided instructions to achieve the victory. Jericho was not handed to Joshua. Joshua had to work for it! Our problem today is that we want to be blessed but don't want to put in the work for the blessing (really let that marinate). We have to adjust our "owe me" mentality to a "let me work for it" mentality.

Too many of us have an attitude that demands we are owed this or that when actually no one owes you anything unless you put in work to equal or exceed what you think should come to you. If you want the blessing of a promotion, you *gotta* work for it! You may have to put in long hours, accept stretched-out assignments, and go above and beyond the call of duty to show that you are worthy of a promotion.

If you want the blessing of a husband or wife, you *gotta* work for him or her! You may have to evaluate yourself to identify your weaknesses, stop running the streets, shut down the bedroom to "visitors," and utilize your season of singleness to strengthen your relationship with God—all the things to prepare you for your mate!

If you want the blessing of a home, you *gotta* work for it! You may have to cut back on your spending, sacrifice only for the things you need, work to get your credit straight so you can get a good interest rate, and work to get your house in order (let that marinate). The list can go on and on. Whatever God promises to you, you *gotta* work for it!

God can bless us anytime He desires, but what good is it to simply give us the blessing if we don't work for it? Oh, and let's not forget that if God simply gave us our blessings, we would view it as our own doing and not glorify Him. So the promise of a blessing and the instructions to get the blessing from God ensure He receives the glory!

There is great joy in seeing the fruits of your hard labor. There is motivation and inspiration in seeing the result of your hard work. There is not as long of an effect of something given to you as much as something you earned. If you want the blessing, you gotta work for it!

SMILE THROUGH THE PAIN

Job 9:27

If you are reading this and going through something, then this is for you! If you are reading this and not going through something, then save this, as it may be encouraging when you are going through something! Oftentimes, people will see your smile and assume that everything is alright. They don't have a clue about the pain you are experiencing. They don't have a clue about the internal tears you are shedding. They don't have a clue about the sleepless nights you are enduring. They don't have a clue as to how hard it is for you to smile while you are going through what you are going through.

If it were not for God on your side, your smile would probably be a consistent frown! If it were not for God on your side, you may have unleashed your pain on someone else! If it were not for God on your side, your mighty tongue would have probably cut down everyone who approached you! When others see your smile, they don't understand the peace of God that has overtaken you and enabled you to smile through the pain.

I finally embraced smiling through my pain after seeing a loved one, who was lying in a hospital bed with a tube in their mouth, smile when I told them that my wife was pregnant with our son. If they could smile through their pain and a tube in their mouth, then I can smile through my pain!

"I hear all that, but you don't know what I am going through. It is hard to smile through this." If you are saying this very statement, I would say you are right! I don't know what you are going through. It is not my business to know what you are going through, but we can encourage each other to smile through the pain. Yes, encourage each other! I will not share this thought and have you thinking that I can't smile through the pain.

I, for one, wear my reality on my face but am trying to put forth effort to smile through the pain. I can testify and those that know me can testify that it has been very hard for me to smile in recent days. It has been hard because of what I am going through. It has been hard because of the painful results of my actions. It has been hard because I understand the pain someone has been feeling as a result of my actions. I'm not ashamed to share my pain in this thought. See, we want to tell others about the good things that happen to us but are afraid to share our stormy days with others, not realizing that even our storms are testimonies that can help others get through what they are going through!

I try to remind myself of God's promise, "Fear not, for I am with you; be not dismayed, for I am your God. I will strengthen you, Yes, I will help you, I will uphold you with My righteous right hand" (Isaiah 41:10). I try to remind myself that God has never failed me, He has never let me down, and He has *always* picked me up when I have been down. I try to remind myself that God would not allow me to endure the pain if I wasn't anointed to handle the pain (let that marinate)!

When I think about the goodness of God, the smile comes alive in the midst of the pain! When I think about how God looked beyond my faults and *still* called me to do an important task in His perfect will, a smile rises out of the pain! When I think about how God brought me out before, a smile appears on my face because I know this, too, shall pass!

You can smile through the pain! I can smile through the pain! We can smile through the pain! You will smile through the pain! I will smile through the pain! We will smile through the pain! The pain may be unbearable! The pain may have you down! But you can smile! We can smile! We will smile! Your smile is not just for you, but it is for others to see God operating in you and through you. Others will be encouraged to smile, too!

Smile—it is a gift from God, and it looks so good on you!

Related Reading

Psalm 31:16; Isaiah 41:10; Philippians 4:7

WHAT ARE YOU TELLING YOURSELF?

Mark 25:28

For a moment, let's reflect back to the account of the woman with the issue of blood. She had been dealing with her issue for a long time; twelve years to be exact. She tried things on her own in terms to find relief for her issue but was not successful. How many of us can relate? We've been dealing with an issue or issues for a period of time and have tried different failed solutions (let that marinate).

When she heard about Jesus, she pushed her way through the crowd to get to Him. Let me stop right there to encourage someone. You have to push through the crowd of your issue and get to Jesus (let that marinate, too). The woman told herself that if she could touch His clothes, she would be made well. Though the woman was in pain, she did not allow her pain to keep her from receiving the healing she so desired! We allow our issue or issues to beat us down, keep us frustrated, and encourage us to give up. What if the woman had had a defeated mindset? What if the woman had said, "I can't be healed"? What if the woman had said it was not worth fighting the crowd to get to Jesus? More than likely, the woman may not have received her healing. See, it was not the touch that healed the woman but her faith in knowing that if she could get to Jesus, she would be healed.

What are you telling yourself in your issue? If I can be blunt but still understanding, we *all* have issues. There is nowhere in the Bible that states that we would not have any issues, any storms, or any trials. I'm not saying that we should go looking for issues but I am saying issues will arise in our lives. I would contend that what you speak into your issue may determine how long you deal with the issue. I would contend that what you think in your issue may determine how much power it will have over you.

Need I remind you that the Word says death and life are in the power of the tongue? We speak death in our issue before we speak life (let that marinate)! What are you telling yourself in your issue? Are you encouraging yourself, or are you helping the issue defeat you? Are you speaking life despite your issue which will cause your issue to die (let that marinate)? Are you activating your faith in your issue, or are you activating yourself (really let that marinate)?

"Well, you don't know what I am going through." If you are saying this, you are already speaking the wrong thing in your storm. Yes, I don't know what you are going through in your storm, but I can encourage you in the storm. God blesses us with the help we need when we need it the most. So, when you are too tired to encourage yourself, He will send someone to encourage you. When Moses grew tired overlooking the battle below, Aaron and Hur raised his arms, and Israel prevailed in battle. As you are going through your issue or issues, speak life and not death! Tell yourself:

"I am an overcomer!"

"I have the *victory* because He gave me the victory!"

"I will not be defeated!"

"Though He slay me, yet will I trust in Him!" (Job 13:15)

"I'm alive in Christ!"

"In *all* that I go through, I am more than a conqueror!"

My brothers and sisters, what are you telling yourself? Think before you speak!

ENCOURAGE YOURSELF

1 Samuel 30:6

You are a child of the great and mighty God! You are anointed! You are a blessing! The enemy does not like it when we remind ourselves about who we are and our connection to the Father. See, the enemy wants you to walk around with your head held down in distress. The enemy wants you to curse the very name you praise! The enemy wants you to speak those things that will cause you to miss your blessing! The enemy doesn't want you to move to your blessing but remain stuck in despair! The enemy wants you to see all your faults, all your mistakes, all your worries, all the things that keep you from Jesus. You will *not* give the enemy what he wants!

God made us in His image, not the image of a dog, cat, whale, or bird but *His* image. Now that's encouraging! He did not give things of the earth authority over us but gave us dominion over the things of the earth! With your power, you have the absolute right to speak life over yourself! The deathly words are nothing more than the enemy's way to further discourage you and pull you away from God. In the name of *Jesus,* rebuke the enemy's attempt and speak life into your situation. Encourage yourself!

I don't care what your situation looks like! I don't even have to understand your situation! If this doesn't speak to anyone else, it is speaking to me! I don't care if you are tired, stressed, worried, or whatever! You take a look at yourself and *you* encourage yourself in the Lord! You are a conqueror and not defeated! You are the head and not the tail! You are above and not beneath! Get up off your rusty dusty, speak positivity into your life, and praise God! If you change what you speak, you can change your atmosphere. Speak life, speak victory, encourage yourself! If you change your outlook, the way you look out will change (let that marinate). Be blessed and stay encouraged!

Related Reading

Proverbs 18:21

THE HUMBLING EXPERIENCE

Luke 15:17-19, 22-24

If you are familiar with the parable of the prodigal son, then you will recall how the son asked his father for his portion of goods and left home. When he had wasted or mistreated his possessions, the prodigal son realized the blessing of being home. The prodigal son realized how good he had it at home. He realized that even his father's servants were in a better position than he was. The prodigal son returned home expecting to be on the level of his father's servants, but his father, a forgiving father, welcomed him back home and restored him to his position. Due to his commitment to his father, the older son did not appreciate the younger brother being welcomed back. But the father acknowledged the transformation of the prodigal son; "For your brother was dead and is alive again, and was lost and is found" (Luke 15:32).

As I was reading the parable of the prodigal son, the Holy Spirit revealed to me that the son had a humbling experience. How many of you have not truly appreciated your blessings? How many of you have taken your blessings for granted? How many of you had to eat humble pie to realize your blessings? How many of you had to go through something to wake you up so you could realize and truly embrace your blessings? I would contend that we can all relate to the prodigal son. I know I can!

It takes an experience to humble you! It takes an experience for you to see the fullness of the blessing bestowed upon you! It takes an experience for you to kill some stuff within you and transform into a new creature. I love the fact that the father did not turn his back on his son. I love the fact that the father did not give his son grief about his actions but acted as if the actions never happened. I love the fact that the father did not treat the son less than a son but restored him to his rightful place. I love the fact that the parable reminds us that our Father will never turn His back on us! I love the fact that our Father will not give us grief about our actions and will forgive our actions when we seek Him for forgiveness! I really love the fact that our Father will not treat us less than who we are and will restore us!

A humbling experience will bring you to your knees! A humbling experience will show you the errors of your ways! A humbling experience will remove the mask and reveal who you are! A humbling experience will kill some things in you so you can transform into a new creature! A humbling experience will give you a greater appreciation for the blessings that you took for granted! A humbling experience will show a lost soul how to return home! When you are humble, God *will* lift you up! When you are humble, God *will* restore you! When you are humble, God *will* bless you!

Embrace your humbling experience! Castor oil doesn't taste good, but it does you some good! Your experience may not feel good, but the experience will humble you for your good (let that marinate)!

Related Reading

James 4:10; 1 Peter 5:6

KEEP P.U.S.H.ING

So you have been praying and feel that your prayers have gone unheard. You have been praying, but you haven't seen any actions as a result of your prayer. You are getting discouraged because you think God is not listening to you. Well, let me encourage you by saying God hears you! Our timing is not God's timing. When we want things to happen may not be God's time for them to happen! Don't think that just because you don't see any change in your situation that God is not listening. Check this out:

> Then he said to me, "Do not fear, Daniel, for from the first day that you set your heart to understand, and to humble yourself before your God, your words were heard' and I have come because of your words. But the prince of the kingdom of Persia withstood me twenty-one days; and behold, Michael, one of the chief princes, came to help me, for I had been left alone there with the kings of Persia. Now I have come to make you understand what will happen to your people in the latter days, for the vision refers to many days yet to come" (Daniel 10:12-14).

See, Daniel was praying and fasting for three weeks (according to the Scripture); hence we have the phrase we use commonly today: "Daniel Fast." In Daniel's case, it wasn't that God didn't hear him; the delay was due to Gabriel being held up in battle (spiritual) and then receiving help from Michael (SN: God will *always* send help when you need it). Gabriel had to fight his way to get to Daniel to deliver the message.

Let me share something with you; you are *so* important that the Kingdom of Light and Kingdom of Darkness are fighting over you! In fighting over you, Satan will send out agents to stop you from receiving a word or blessing. But we all know that Satan can't win! We serve a great and mighty God! The battle is not ours but the Lord's, and because it is His battle, victory is ours!

Be encouraged! Stay focused! Keep praying as you wait on the

Lord. He hears you and *will* answer you! A delay is not a denial! "Weeping may endure for a night, but joy will come in the morning (Psalm 30:5). Hold on for your morning and experience the joy of God!! Keep Praying Until Something Happens!

SHUT UP AND BE BLESSED

Luke 1:13-20

The biblical account of Zacharias and Elizabeth is one of my favorites to read. The couple was righteous in their relationship with God; they were blameless and walked in His commandments. Elizabeth was barren, and both of them were advanced in years. Regardless of their age or Elizabeth's situation, God heard Zacharias' prayer and promised the birth of a son.

Zacharias heard the promise but questioned the promise. It can be perceived that the promise was questioned because of the timing of it. Zacharias was old. In order for the promise to be fulfilled, Zacharias was made mute until it came to pass. The promise eventually manifested! Sometimes, we have to be muted or shut up until the promise is fulfilled (I'm letting this marinate).

Oftentimes, we submit a request to God through prayer believing in the word "Ask and it shall be given to you" but will question the very request we submitted for one reason or another (Matt. 7:7, KJV). We may question it to the point of not believing it will be fulfilled. Better yet, we speak death to our request before it is formed and birthed from the spiritual womb (let that marinate). May I take it a step further? Even *after* the blessing is received, we can run our mouth so much that it can lead to losing the very blessing that we prayed for day in and day out (really let that marinate).

Loose lips sink ships! There is a time to speak, and there is a time to simply shut up! If nobody receives this message, I receive it! If this message does not speak to anyone else, I am not afraid nor ashamed to say it is definitely speaking to me at this very moment! Even as I type out these words, the Holy Spirit is telling me to be quiet and let God have His way! The Holy Spirit is saying your words are working against the work of God and delaying progress! The Holy Spirit is saying if you believe God will fix it, then close your mouth and receive it!

If you submit a request to God, then believe it will come to pass! Be patient and wait for it! Abraham waited 25 years for the fulfillment of God's promise to him, and he remained faithful to Him during the waiting period (let that marinate, too). Whatever you ask of God, it will happen at the right time: His time! In the meantime, keep your mouth shut so you don't talk yourself out of your blessing! Shut up and be blessed!

"BUT" PRAISE

Psalm 30:5

In conjunction form, the term "but" is used to introduce something that contrasts with what has already been mentioned. I like to think that anything that comes before "but" is negated or canceled by the action that follows it. In the context verse above, it says that weeping endures for a night, but joy comes in the morning. Though the psalmist was experiencing a moment of weeping, he knew that joy is everlasting. Maybe the psalmist was experiencing a painful night sleeping but knew relief would come in the morning!

Words are powerful! The words we use can speak life into our situations or kill our situations! The words we use can build up and tear down! The words we speak can be motivational or depressing! The words we speak can result in receiving a blessing or blocking a blessing (let that marinate)! Proverbs 18:21 says, "Death and life are in the power of the tongue, and those who love it will eat its fruit." If you don't believe this Scripture is true, keep living!

The tongue should not be taken lightly. James 3:8-9 says, "But no man can tame the tongue. It is an unruly evil, full of deadly poison. With it we bless our God and Father, and with it we curse men, who have been made in the similitude of God."

So what am I saying? I am glad you asked that question! We can use the power of our tongues to cancel out the attacks of the enemy! We can use the power of our tongues to change our situations! We can use the power of our tongues to change our atmospheres! Despite how things may look, enter into a "but" praise. That's right, a "but" praise:

"I may be struggling financially, *but* it will change!"

"People may have discredited me, *but* God's credit is all I need!"

"I may not have a job, *but* God will promote me into a better position!"

"I may be weak, *but* my God will restore my strength!"

"Satan, you may have me down for the moment, *but* God will lift me up!"

"I may have fallen, *but* God will pick me up!"

"I may be in the storm, *but* I will praise my way out!"

"It's been a long, rainy journey, *but* sunlight is on the way!"

"The enemy can throw everything at me, *but* I will still praise the Lord!"

"Things may not be going well right now, *but* it will get better through Christ Jesus!"

"I may be sick now, *but* by His stripes, I am healed!"

"I may be enduring some bad days, *but* good days are on the way!"

"Weeping may endure for a night, *but* joy comes in the morning!"

"I may be going through hardships, *but* God!"

Despite what you may be going through and no matter your circumstances, you got a reason to praise God! You could have been dead and gone, sleeping in your grave, but God woke you up this morning and that is a reason to praise Him!! Every day God allows us to see is a reason to praise Him! Every day God allows us to re-write our wrongs from yesterday is a reason to praise Him! You are able to read this thought; that is a reason to praise God!

Your co-workers, family, and friends may get on your nerves (and I'm quite sure you get on their nerves, too), but there are some who don't have anyone to get on their nerves because they are physically alone in this world. You are not physically alone, and that is a reason to praise God. He has kept you from dangers seen and unseen and closed doors that were not for you; these are reasons for you to praise God! With everything that you have been through so far in your life, you still have life, so you have a reason to praise God!

I could go on and on, but the common denominator is you got a reason to praise God! Your praise is *not* a Sealy Posturepedic, so stop sleeping on it (let that marinate)! Your praise tells God that you appreciate what He has done for you! Your praise tells God that you appreciate what He is doing in the season! Your praise tells God that you appreciate what He will do in your life! Your praise tells God that you appreciate Him for being Him! God is the reason for your praise! Don't hold back what He so rightfully deserves; give Him your praise!

It's time to stop speaking about our situations and start speaking to our situations! It's time to stop complaining about our situations and start praising in our situations! Your "but" praise can turn things around! Don't take my word for it; show your situation your "but" and see what happens for yourself!

GOD, FIGHT FOR ME

2 Chronicles 20:15-17

My brothers and sisters, how many of you are in the midst of a fight? You are fighting for your finances! You are fighting for peace on the job! You are fighting depression! You are fighting addiction! You are fighting for your marriage! You are fighting for your health! You are fighting for someone or something that may not return the favor and fight for you!

You are fighting and have been fighting for quite some time now. As soon as you think you are winning, you endure a setback. As soon as you think you've made a winning move, you are pushed back. As soon as you think you can celebrate a win, your hopes are dashed by something that took you by surprise. Now, you are to the point where you believe you can't win. You are at the point of thinking that you won't win. You are at the point of exhaustion! You are at the point of giving up because you have no more to give to the fight! But don't give up because you will win!

"I will win? You don't know the fight I am in or how long I have been fighting!" You are exactly right! Yes, you will win! No, I don't know the fight that you are in or how long you have been fighting! Here is the problem, which applies to me, too. You have been fighting the fight! I have been fighting the fight! *We* have been fighting a fight that we should have given to *God!*

He prepared us to stand in the fight, not fight the fight! Ephesians 6:13 says, "Therefore take up the whole armor of God, that you may be able to withstand in the evil day, having done all, to stand." He trained us to stay in the fight but not fight the fight!

Daniel 3:25 says, "'Look!' he answered, 'I see four men loose, walking in the midst of the fire, and they are not hurt, and the form of the fourth is like the Son of God.'" He told us to stand still in the fight to see His salvation!

In 2 Chronicles 20:17, He tells us to position ourselves, stand still, and see the salvation of the Lord who is with us! He didn't tell us to position ourselves, fight, and see His salvation! He told us to position ourselves and stand still! See, our problem is we don't want to stand still! We don't want to surrender our ways for His ways! We want to be in control instead of letting Him have control of our fight!

I don't know about you, but I am tired of fighting! I don't know about you, but I don't have any more fight left in me! I don't know about you, but this is what I am going to do! I am not going to fight a fight that I can't fight! I'm giving the fight to God! I am casting the fight upon Him and will let Him fight it for me! I am giving my fight to God so I can rest because He promised me rest! I am giving my fight to God because I don't have what it takes to fight this fight like God! I am giving my fight to God and will stand still until He tells me to move! I am going to show up to the fight with God on my side but let God take the lead in the fight!

See, I serve a Winner! We serve a Winner! God is undefeated! He has a perfect record and has never lost a fight! He doesn't win by unanimous decisions but by TKOs! Rocky Balboa had the eye of the tiger to encourage him! Well, I have the eye of God to encourage me! I have the power of God as my assurance that the fight has been won! I have the glory of God to praise as He fights my fight! I have a humble heart to ask God to fight for me!

You can't do it! I can't do it! We can't do it! But God can and God will! God, fight for me!

Related Reading

Matthew 11:28; 1 Peter 5:6-7

HELP IN THE BATTLE

Exodus 17:8-13

If you are familiar with this account, Joshua and the army are fighting the Amalekites while Moses, Aaron, and Hur are on the top of the hill overlooking the battle. When Moses raised his hands, Israel prevailed. When Moses let down his hands, the Amalekites (the enemy) prevailed. Moses's hands became heavy, so Aaron and Hur sat him on a stone and supported his hands on each side, Aaron on one side and Hur on the other. They supported Moses's hands to keep them up, and Joshua defeated the Amalekites.

There are two things from this passage that serve as a reminder that we will always have help in our battles. The first thing is God will always provide help when we are weary or tired. Aaron and Hur helped Moses when he was unable to hold up his own hands. God will always position someone to help us when we are tired or ready to quit! The second thing is you are not winning the battle because of your own will; you are winning because someone is outside of the battle praying to God on your behalf.

As Joshua was down in the valley fighting, Moses was up on the hill with outstretched arms to God. All Joshua knew was that Moses would be on the top of the hill but didn't know what he would be doing. All we need to know is that while we are in the battle and winning, someone must be on the outside praying on our behalf!

If you are in a "battle" right now, be encouraged in knowing that God will provide the help you need to win the battle! If you are tired, He will provide! If you are weary, He will provide! If you are weak, He will provide! If you are frustrated, He will provide! And remember, you are never alone because someone is always praying for your victory in battle! Keep fighting; don't give up! You have help in the battle!

HE SEES THE BEST IN YOU

But the Lord said to Samuel, "Do not look at his appearance or at his physical stature, because I have refused him. For the Lord does not see as man sees; for man looks at the outward appearance, but the Lord looks at the heart" (1 Samuel 16:7)

"For My thoughts are not your thoughts, nor are your ways My ways," says the Lord. "For as the heavens are higher than the earth, so are My ways higher than your ways, and My thoughts than your thoughts" (Isaiah 55:8-9)

Have you ever been counted out? Have you ever felt that you were passed over for someone else (relationship, promotion, etc.)? Did anyone doubt your abilities? Did people say you would never amount to anything? Have people made false assumptions about you simply because of your appearance? Are you struggling with your self-esteem? Are you afraid to hold your head up high when thinking about what others have to say about you? Let me help you. God sees the best in you!

The account of David being chosen as Saul's successor is a great reminder of how God views us and an example of how we should view others. I can only imagine seven tall, muscular men standing before Samuel eagerly waiting to see if they were the anointed one. By appearance, they probably thought they were the anointed one. I can only imagine the astonished look upon the faces of the seven tall, muscular men when the oil fell upon their younger brother David. You know David, the young boy who would later stand fearless before Goliath and bring him down through his faith. Even Goliath laughed at the appearance of the young lad, but it was David who had the last laugh.

Your "best" does not rest on the outside but on the inside. Your appearance is merely a shell or mask hiding the treasure that lies within. If you simply go by the "packaging," you will miss the blessed gift (let that marinate). Our problem is we tend to judge a person by what they look like and not what they bring to the table. If a person doesn't fit our model or ideas, we dismiss them. We assume that if a person is not like us, then something is wrong with them when, in reality, they are serving as a mirror to our soul (let that marinate, too). I don't think I have to say what happens when you assume (you already know).

If you or someone you know is struggling with "self," having a hard time with self-acceptance, battling self-esteem issues, or simply questioning self-worth, allow this message to serve as a reminder that God sees the best in you and that other person! Do you know why God sees the best in you? He sees the best in you because The Best is in you! We are created in *His* image, the best image! Genesis 1:26a says, "Then God said, 'Let Us make man in Our image, according to Our likeness.'" Genesis 2:7 says, "And the Lord God formed man of the dust of the ground, and breathed into his nostrils the breath of life; and man became a living being."

It does not matter what man does to you, thinks about you, or says about you. It does not matter if you have fallen, messed up, or made mistakes. It does not matter if people write you off like a bad debt; your credit is always good with God. Why? He sees you for who you are; He sees the best in you!

GOD HAS HIS HANDS ON YOU

Isaiah 41:13; 64:8

This is a word that was shared in 2017 and is still needed for to-day! You need to be reminded that God has His hands on you! I need to be reminded that God has His hands on me! Despite what you may be going through, God has His hands on you! It doesn't feel good to be in what we are in right now, but God has His hands on you! He is allowing you and me to go through what we are going through because He has His hands on us! We are able to walk among the "lions" on the job because God has His hands on us! We are able to be in the fire and come out without a mark because He has His hands on us protecting us from the fire! God has His hands on you! God has His hands on me!

He knows what we are going through! He knows the pain we are enduring! He knows the obstacles that we are facing! He knew what we were going to go through before we got to it! He is the Alpha and Omega, the Beginning and the End! He is the Author of lives, and be-cause He knows our stories, His hands are on us throughout every chapter of our lives. In all things, He has His hands on you!

You may ask "Lord, why me?" or "Lord, why am I going through this?" Just as He trusted Job to go through, He trusts you, too! He has faith in you and keeps His hands on you! The uncomfortable feeling you are experiencing may not be what you think. He is the Potter, and we are His clay. The uncomfortable feeling, pruning of unnecessary things, the hurt and pain, and the removal of people could be the result of His hands shaping and molding you (let that marinate).

Others will see you going through and wonder how you are mak-ing it through! Others will see you smile through the pain and wonder why you are able to smile! Others will see you and wonder how you are able to do what you are able to do! The answer? Because God has His hands on you! When they realize the hands of God are upon you and embrace the fact that God's hands are on them, then they will be encouraged, inspired to work with God's hands and not against God's hands (let that marinate).

So you may be going through it, you may not feel good, you may be tired (don't give up) but know that just like Allstate Insurance, you *are* in good hands! I can smile because God has His hands on me! I can keep pushing because God has His hands on me! I can cry because God has His hands on me! I can rejoice because God has His hands on me! I know that I will be alright because God has His hands on me!

And guess what? You will be alright, too! God has His hands on you!

NO WEAPON FORMED WILL PROSPER

Isaiah 54:16-17a

God created each of us for a divine Kingdom purpose. He created *all* things for a purpose. As I read the Scripture, I considered that even Satan himself was made for a purpose but decided to operate in his own. God still uses him for *His* purpose anyway (read Romans 8:28).

We have to understand that if God said it, it shall be! If God said it, then it will be! When God speaks, the word is birthed! When God speaks, the blessing is birthed! When God speaks, something happens! When God speaks, what He says *shall* be!

Isaiah 55:11 says, "So shall My word be that goes forth from My mouth; it shall not return to Me void. But it shall accomplish what I please, and it shall prosper in the thing for which I sent it."

God promised Himself, not you, not me, that whatever He says, it will be! And because He said it will be, there is no devil in hell that can stop God's will from prospering! There is no devil in hell that can stop the manifestation of God's Word! There is no devil in hell that can stop you from seeing the blessings God promised you! There is no devil in hell that can stop God from using you for His purpose! There is no devil in hell that can stop the mighty works of God!

Satan could not cause harm to Job without God's permission, and even his actions were limited. It wasn't about Job but about God when Satan attempted to convince Job to turn from God through the attacks on him. Guess what? What you are going through is not about you, and what I go through is not about me but about God (let that marinate)! The weapons targeted toward Job did not succeed! And the weapons used to attack you will not succeed!

Satan may create the weapon, but it can't win! Satan may create the weapon, but it won't succeed! Satan may send his agents to consume those close to you, but their efforts will not prosper! Satan may mess with your finances, but his effort will be effortless! Satan may send a wedge to cause division in your home, school, church, or workplace, but it will not prosper! No weapon formed against us shall prosper because the power of the weapon is limited! No weapon formed against us shall prosper because God is *always* in control! No weapon formed against us shall prosper because the will of God cannot be stopped!

No weapon formed against you shall prosper!

IT WILL WORK FOR YOUR GOOD

Romans 8:28

How many of you know that all things work for your good? As the song says, how many of you know that God is intentional? The artist said, "Everything is working together for my good." Oftentimes, we allow our storms, issues, trials, and circumstances influence us into thinking that things can't get better or won't get better. We allow our perception of our situation to discourage us! We walk around stressed or depressed because we feel that there is no way out. We walk around with our heads held down disregarding that we are more than conquerors and that conquerors walk with their heads held up high! Well, today, change your stinking thinking! Today, get off your rusty dusty and exercise your faith!

"How can you tell me to change my thinking when you don't know what I am going through? Who are you to tell me to exercise my faith?" As brothers and sisters in Christ, we should encourage one another, build each other up, and remind each other of the One who is *always* in control! You are *not* the only one going through something! You will not be the only one going through something!

I can tell you to change your thinking because if the change worked for me, then it will work for you, too! I can tell you to exercise your faith because if it worked for me, then it will work for you, too! I may not know what you are going through, but I know Who will pull you through! I may not know what you are going through, but I know Who has a master plan that trumps the plans of the enemy. I may not know what you are going through, but I know Who has a purpose for you. His purpose will be fulfilled. It will work for your good!

When we mess up, God has a way of cleaning up our mess to work for His good. Even when we take a wrong turn and cause a delay in reaching our blessing, He uses that delay to teach us a lesson, recalculate our steps, and prepare us for our blessing. We have to embrace and understand that God has a purpose for each of us, and no matter what happens in our lives, things *will* work out for our good! How do I know this? When it appeared that things were not going to work out in my life, He stepped in and worked them out! When I stumbled and wanted to end it all (real talk), His purpose for my life trumped my action to take away my life.

Do you want another reason why I know it will work for your good? God loved us so much that He gave His only Son to die for our salvation, for our good! He made the ultimate sacrifice for us! Funny, God made the ultimate sacrifice for *our* salvation, but we can't sacrifice 10% of our time to Him or give back what He has given to us (I will leave that alone…let it marinate).

If you truly love God, then be encouraged in knowing that whatever you are going through will work out for your good! Isaiah 55:11 says, "'So shall My word be that goes forth from My mouth; It shall not return to Me void, but it shall accomplish what I please, and it shall prosper in the thing for which I sent it.'" You are "the called," and it *will* work out for your good! It will work out because the purpose spoken by God over your life *will* be fulfilled because His words do not produce empty results!

So today, stand strong in the midst of your storm and say, "It's good, it's good, it's good, it's working for my good!" If you won't speak it, then I will speak it for you! You best believe that I am definitely speaking it for myself! "I don't care what it may look like; it *will* work and is working for your good!"

Hold on, my brothers; hold on, my sisters. It is working out for your good!

Related Reading

John 3:16

LED TO LEARN

Exodus 13:17-18

One of the simplest and powerful prayers you can pray is "Lord, open my heart so I may understand the Scripture." This prayer reflects Luke 24:45, "And He opened their understanding, that they might comprehend the Scriptures." I would contend that when you are open to receive the Scripture, a preached word, or revelation from the Holy Spirit, your spiritual roots grow deeper within Him.

Last week, when I read the Scripture above, it was read from a delayed perspective. Our delays have a purpose. While I was watching Tyler Perry's *Love Thy Neighbor,* Mama Hattie made a very strong, profound statement that woke up my spirit. To paraphrase her words, she said, "Sometimes, God allows you to go a certain way to teach you a lesson." Immediately, the Holy Spirit led me back to Exodus 13:17-18.

God could have led the children of Israel down a short path to the promised land. However, He decided to lead them in a different, longer way which was filled with an abundance of lessons. For example, the children of Israel complained about being in the wilderness. Even though they complained and God heard their complaints, He still provided for them in their wilderness moment as a reminder that He is God. No matter what it looks like, God is *always* in control (let that marinate).

Sometimes, we are allowed to go a certain way so God can teach us lessons to help us realize that we have to get some stuff (or people) out of our systems before we can receive our blessings. Sometimes, we are allowed to go a certain way so God can teach us lessons about faith. Sometimes, we are allowed to go a certain way so God can teach us lessons about love. Sometimes, we are allowed to go a certain way so God can remind us that He is God and will never leave nor forsake us. Sometimes, we are allowed to go a certain way so God can use us as the vessel to teach others a valuable lesson necessary for them. Sometimes, we are allowed to go a certain way so God can teach the enemy a lesson about your faithfulness to Him; remaining faithful to Him no matter what the enemy does to you teaches us a lesson about trust.

Based on our journeys thus far, we can name countless lessons that God has taught us. The main thing to remember is your steps are ordered by God. Psalm 37:23-24 says, "The steps of a good man are ordered by the Lord, and He delights in his way. Though he fall, he shall not be utterly cast down; for the Lord upholds him with His hand." Embrace Proverbs 3:5-6, which says, "Trust in the Lord with all your heart, and lean not on your own understanding; in all your ways acknowledge Him, and He shall direct your paths." We are allowed to go a certain way so we can be taught a lesson necessary for our blessing.

Keep your heart and spirit open to the Word and His command so you can comprehend the lesson designed specifically for you. Oh, I almost forgot. Every lesson is followed by a test. Whether it is a pop quiz, short answer, essay, or comprehensive, you will be tested to determine if you fully comprehend the lesson. The outcome could result in you moving to the next level or repeating the same "grade" (hmmm, how many times have you repeated the same thing in life? Let that marinate). Your journey is not by happenstance but necessary so a lesson can be learned!

TO GOD BE THE GLORY

John 11:3-6; 21

During your meditation time, I would highly recommend that you go back and read the account of Jesus raising Lazarus from the dead (John 11:1-44). I recommend that you go back to read the account because all of us will have a "Lazarus" experience. What do I mean? I would hope that all of us would go to God in prayer to pour out our hearts, let Him hear our cries, and release our innermost thoughts to Him. I would hope that all of us would give our problems to God in prayer.

Once we say our prayer, then we wait for Him to move in our situation. We wait for a sign that our prayer has been answered. We wait for confirmation that our prayer has been heard. With each passing day, we wait with anticipation! With each passing day, we wait eagerly for a response! With each passing day, our faith is tested by the waiting!

But then, something happens in our situation that causes us to go to God and question why He didn't move fast enough. Something happens in our situation and we question whether or not our prayer was heard because the outcome is not a reflection of the answer we were seeking from our prayer. Something happens in our situation to lead us to believe that it is over! Well, my brothers and sisters, what we see as a dead outcome is only the beginning for God!

Jesus knew Lazarus was sick but did not run to his side. I would contend that he didn't run to Lazarus's side when he was sick because the glory of God would be bigger in death than life (let that marinate). The impact of going to Lazarus after death was greater than going to him while he was sick. Jesus went to him when He was ready and not when man wanted Him to go (let that marinate, too).

To Martha and Mary, the situation was dead! They said to Jesus, "If You had been here, my brother would not have died." How many times have you said "Jesus, if You had been here?" "Jesus, if You had been here, my heart would not have been broken!" "Jesus, if You had been here, sickness would not have invaded my body!" "Jesus, if You had been here, my marriage would still be intact." "Jesus, if You had been here, I wouldn't have lost my peace on my job!"

We say to Jesus, "If You had been here," but Jesus claps back (as the young people say) to let us know that He didn't come when we wanted Him to, but He's here now when we need Him the most!! See, it is not about you or me! It is not about what we want right now! It is about the Father and Son who are glorified while we are going through what we are going through! It is about the Father and Son who are glorified after we go through what we have been through! To God be the glory!

Beloved, your "Lazarus" situation is *not* dead! The situation on your job is *not* dead! The situation with your family is *not* dead! The situation with your finances is *not* dead! The situation with your health is not dead! The situation with your marriage is not dead! It is not over! Hallelujah! I don't care what you are going through! I don't care what I am going through! You may feel like you are down to the last count, but it is *not* over!

Jesus has the final say! Jesus has the final say! Jesus has the final say! You didn't think you were going to make it, but Jesus has the final say! Man said you weren't going to make it, but Jesus has the final say! If Jesus can raise Lazarus from the tomb, then He can raise you from your "tomb" (let that marinate)! If Jesus can restore life to Lazarus, then He can restore life to your situation! If Jesus can free Lazarus from death, then He can most certainly free you from your situation!

So, keep pushing! Keep pressing! To God be the glory because it is *not* over!!

YOU ARE BLESSED, SO STOP COMPLAINING

Exodus 16:11-12

The word today is straight forward; you *are* blessed, so stop complaining! The children of Israel complained about their wilderness situation. They were brought out of a bad situation but still complained. It is sad that no matter what we do for others or, better yet, what God does for us, we still find a reason to complain. We are never satisfied. God gives us the gift of life *every* morning, yet we complain about getting up to go to a place of His provision (let that marinate).

God opened the door for us to walk into our jobs by touching the heart of the hiring manager to hire us and keeping us there for as long as we have been there, yet we complain about the blessing of having a job. I could go on and on. The end result is that we need to stop complaining about the blessings of God and praise Him more, not just for the blessings but because He is God!

We complain about having a job when there are some who would love to have a job! We complain about having little money when there are some who would love to have some money instead of no money! We complain about getting up at a given time to go to work, school, or wherever, but there are some who will never rise from their position (let that marinate)! We complain about the increased prices of things such as gas, food, etc. when there are less fortunate people who go without every day!

We complain about being in a worship service anywhere from two hours to all day on Sunday but don't complain about the hell we entertain Monday through Saturday (yeah, I said it and am guilty myself... let that deeply marinate)! We complain about the actions of our child or children, but there are some who will never experience parenthood! We complain about the actions of our spouse, but there are some who have buried their spouses or never had the blessing of a spouse! I would contend that our complaints are self-centered as we only consider ourselves in the complaint and don't take others into consideration.

Before you complain, stand still and remember what God has done for you! Before you complain, stand still and say, "Thank You, God, for what You are doing right now!" Before you complain, stand still and think about where you could have been if it were *not* for the God on your side! Before you complain, stand still and think about those who don't have what you have (a job, some money, a family, food, shelter, education, clothes, good health, etc.)!

Before you complain, stand still and remember that if God brought you out of "Egypt" before, then He will bring you out again! Before you complain, stand still and give thanks, for the thanks you give will shift the atmosphere to usher in peace instead of the mess brought on through complaining! Before you complain, stand still and remember that all things work together for good to those who love God, to those who are the called according to His purpose (Rom. 8:28)!

When you spend more time complaining, being ungrateful, speaking negatively, etc. versus praising and giving thanks, the enemy has you right where he wants you. See, the Word says in John 10:10, "The thief does not come except to steal, and to kill, and to destroy. I have come that they may have life, and that they may have it more abundantly." When you complain, you allow the enemy to steal your joy, your peace. When you complain, you allow the enemy to kill your hope, your motivation, your situation. When you complain, you allow the enemy to destroy your faith. Our complaining gives the enemy a shimmer of hope that we may turn away from God.

Here is the good news! Despite our complaints, God blesses us anyway! When we are not thankful for our blessings, He keeps on blessing us anyway! He looks beyond our "noise pollution" and continues to be our Provider anyway! Our complaints don't and won't stop the goodness of God! He will continue to be God regardless of our complaints. Why? Because it is *not* about you or me but about Him!

The only thing our complaints do is give the enemy a shimmer of hope that we may turn from God; they are a praise session that is music to the enemy's ears. So why complain? I've had some good days. I've had some hills to climb. I've had some weary days and some sleepless nights. But when I look around and think things over, all of my good days outweigh my bad days! I won't complain!

From this day forward, let's make a conscious effort to stop complaining. Why? Because we are *blessed!* Enough said!

Related Reading

Exodus 14:13-14

TIME TO TAKE IT BACK

John 10:10a

How many of you have experienced a period of time in which your days were sunny and, all of a sudden, dark clouds rolled in attempting to steal your joy? How many of you are experiencing battles on your job or in your home? How many of you feel like every time you take one step forward you go two steps backward? Spiritual warfare is no joke and is intense. It can bring you to the point of discouragement or depression and can even make you want to give up or turn away from God.

The battle will raise up thoughts that lead you to question why or maybe question God. Even in your weary moments, it is important that you call on the name of Jesus, for when you are weak, He is strong! It is His power which gives us the victory over Satan's attacks! If you haven't experienced an attack, keep living because you will, and it won't be just one but will be many.

The Word says, "The thief does not come except to steal, and to kill, and to destroy" (John 10:10a). It is not hard for the enemy to accomplish this feat when we willingly give him our stuff. We give the enemy our joy when faced with adversities. We give the enemy praise with our complaints. We give the enemy our peace when we are in the midst of a storm. We leave the door cracked wide enough for the enemy to come in and wreak havoc in our lives. We leave the window to our lives open so the enemy can peek inside and see what kind of damage he can do. We let down our guard and let the enemy enter our thoughts, our hearts, and our spirits and influence us to do some crazy stuff. Today, its time take it back!!

Message to the enemy:

"I may have given it to you, but God is going to give it back to me. God will restore my joy! God will restore my peace! God will restore my happiness! God will renew my faith! God will strengthen my faith! God will restore my dominion over you! God has brought to my remembrance that I am *more than a conqueror!* Though you slay me, yet I will trust in Him! The battle is not mine but the Lord's, so victory is *mine!*

"Just as the walls of Jericho fell down, you will fall to the hands of my Father! Just as David stood before Goliath in the name of the Lord of hosts and he (Goliath) was delivered to David, I stand before you in the name of God, and He will deliver everything you have taken from me back to me! Everything that you may have stolen and anything that was given to you will be given back to me!"

Today is the day that you get back what was taken from you! Take back your life! Take back your finances! Take back yourself! The great force of God will repossess what was taken from or given by you back to you!! *This is the day* that you take back the control submissively given to the enemy! It's time to take back what the enemy has forcefully taken from you! It's time to take back what you have allowed the enemy to take from you!

Take back your peace! Take back your joy! Take back your happiness! Take back your strength! Take back your home! Take back your family! Take back your husband! Take back your wife! Take back your children! Take back your good health! Take back your workplace! Take back your authority! Take it back, take it back, take it back, take it *all* back! You serve a great and mighty God who can take back what belongs to you!

Related Reading

Ephesians 6:12

SPEAK WISELY, LIFE NOT DEATH

Proverbs 18:21 (NLT)

Speaking your mind is *not* always a good thing. As the Word says, "To everything there is a season, a time for every purpose under heaven" (Eccles. 3:1). There is a time to speak and a time to shut up! You can have the right intentions, but your timing could be wrong. You can have the right motive but the wrong order! The words you speak could push someone over the edge or save them from going over the edge! The words you speak could set a situation ablaze or put the blaze out! The words you speak may do more harm than good or move harm out of the way! "I'm going to say what's on my heart." "I'm going to speak what's on my mind." We say those statements to justify saying what we want to say but don't realize the enemy is waiting to grab hold of the words we speak to cause confusion, stress, verbal altercations, etc.

Think about the times when you said something that made a situation worse! Think about the times when others said something to you that made you feel like dirt or lower than dirt! Think about the times your words killed a dream or hindered a blessing. Think about how you spoke badly over your child or children and they became the words you spoke (let that marinate). Think about how you proclaimed your faith but spoke words that contradicted your faith (let that marinate, too).

On the flip side, think about the time when the doctor gave you a bad report and you spoke, "By His stripes, I am healed!" Think about when you spoke in faith that God would supply your needs and your needs were supplied! Think about when you spoke, "No weapon formed against me shall prosper" when the enemy was attacking your family, your marriage, your wallet, etc. and the attack stopped!

If you don't have anything good to say, then don't say anything at all. Before your mouth writes a check it can't cash, pray for guidance and wisdom so the right words can be taken to the bank (let that marinate). Speak wisely—life not death!

Please join me in prayer:

"Lord, thank You for another day. Forgive us for the words that flow from our mouths and speak against Your will. Forgive us for the thoughts that we release which worsen a situation. Lord, bridle our tongues so we may speak those things that represent You. Death and life are in the power of the tongue, so, Lord, help us to speak life and stop killing things with our words. May the fruit of our lips be sweet to the hearers of the words. May our words be acceptable in Thy sight and pleasing to Thy heart. Before we release any negative things into the atmosphere, Lord, please hold our tongues or send Your angels to halt our speech so we don't mess up Your will. These and other blessings we ask in Your Son Jesus's name. Amen!"

Related Reading

Proverbs 10:19-21 (NLT); Psalm 34:13; James 3:5-6

HAND IT OVER TO GOD

1 Peter 5:6-7

In life, we will encounter things within our control and things out of our control. It is the things out of our control that we try to control which only make matters worse. It is the things out of our control that control our mind! It is the things out of our control that blur our vision! It is the things out of our control that drain our energy! It is the things out of our control that consume our time! I don't know about you, but I am ready to reclaim my time!

I would contend that we have to realize that some of those things out of our control are spiritual and require spiritual intervention. You are losing sleep because you don't have control over your situation! You are stressing because you can't wrap your arms around the situation! You are losing weight or hair because you are thinking too much about the situation outside of your control. Your family, friends, and co-workers are receiving backlash undeservingly from you because you don't have control over your storm! You are at your wit's end, and there is only one thing left to do—hand it over to God!

The Word says, "Casting all your care upon Him, for He cares for you" (1 Peter 5:7). It is not a feel-good statement but the truth. When you hand over your situation to God, you are acknowledging that the battle is not yours to fight but for God to win! When you hand over your situation to Jesus, you are acknowledging that the weight is too heavy for you to carry and that He will carry it for you so you can rest! When you hand over your storm to Jesus, you are acknowledging He will speak to the troubling winds and they will cease from blowing! When you hand over your situation to God, you are surrendering "self" and allowing Him to step into it!

There is a key to handing your storm, your situation, your circumstance, your stress, your anger, your frustration, etc. over to God. *You* are the key in handing over your situation to God! God can do any and *everything,* but I believe He waits for us to go to Him in faith before He moves in our situation. "I can't" or "It's hard to let go" are statements that the enemy wants you to say to contradict the faith you proclaim when days are good or on Sunday mornings (let that marinate). Don't contradict your faith but increase your faith that God will take care of you! Didn't He take care of you before? Well, He can do it again! Move yourself out of the way so God can have His way!

Simply put, let it go, let "them" go! Stop trying to deal with your situation alone and hand it over to God!

Related Reading

2 Chronicles 20:15; Matthew 11:28

IN THE MIDDLE OF EVERYTHING

Matthew 27:38

Good Friday is observed or remembered as the day Jesus Christ sacrificed His life on Calvary by way of crucifixion. He died so *we* may live! He sacrificed His life for our salvation! He carried a cross, our troubles, our issues, our sins, and died on the cross. He carried a cross that would be too heavy for us to carry (let that marinate). When He died, our troubles died! When He died, our wrongdoings died!

Jesus's death is good news! Jesus's resurrection is good news! Through His death, we died to sin. Through His resurrection, we live in obedience to God. In my worldly opinion, Jesus's death and resurrection gave me a new meaning of baptism in the sense that being submerged under water signifies the death of the impure, ungodly things in us, and rising out of the water signifies the resurrection and transformation of a new creature.

The four Gospels—Matthew, Mark, Luke, and John—give us different perspectives of Jesus's ministry. Again, their perspectives were different, but their Subject was the same. I would contend that the four accounts give us good news about Jesus. "Gospel" is often a reference that means "good news."

I want to point out some "good news" which was the same in all accounts. Sometimes, it is good to do a deep-dive analysis to uncover the treasure of the Scripture, and in other cases, the treasure is right in front of you ready to be taken. In each of the Scriptures, we get a description of the scene on Calvary. Two criminals were crucified along with Jesus. In one account, one of the criminals rebuked the other criminal for speaking blasphemy to Jesus (see Luke 23:39-43).

The criminal knew he deserved his punishment but recognized that it was not just for Jesus to be crucified. He asked Jesus to remember him when He entered into His Kingdom, and Jesus gave the criminal entry into the Kingdom that very moment. This confirms it is never too late to seek forgiveness for your sins (let that marinate). That is only part of the good news.

The good news to be shared with you today is unspoken but very significant. All accounts tell us that there was a criminal on each side of Jesus. The accounts do not say to the left of Jesus was one criminal and to the left of that criminal was another criminal. The accounts do not say to the right of one criminal was another criminal and to the right of that criminal was Jesus. The accounts tell us that a criminal was on each side of Jesus. John makes it very plain that Jesus was in the center (I think someone may be shouting already).

The good news is Jesus will *always* be at the center of everything! Jesus is in the eye of your storm; there is peace in the eye of the storm! In times of joy, Jesus is present. In times of sadness, Jesus is present. Remember, no matter what you are going through, Jesus will always be present. You can go through because Jesus is with you! Jesus is and will always be in the middle of everything!

Related Reading

Mark 15:27; Luke 23:32-33; John 19:17-18

HE'S ABLE SO LET THE POWER WORK!

Ephesians 3:20

Ephesians 3:20 is one of my favorite Scriptures because it is a constant reminder that God is able to do what He said He would do and exceed my thoughts, my expectations, my wants, and my needs! Deitrick Haddon, a well-known gospel recording artist, has a song titled "He's Able" that encompasses the words from this Scripture. God is able to do what He said He will do, but I would contend what He does depends on us.

What do you mean? We will acknowledge the Power in us but limit the Power through our actions. See, the Scripture simply says that God is "able to do exceedingly abundantly above all that we ask or think according to the power that works in *us.*" Let's be totally honest; we don't allow the Power to work consistently in us or all the time. A prime example is that we spend most of our time in the workplace. In our respective jobs, we face issues, encounter obstacles, combat stress, etc. We become extremely frustrated and ready to jump ship.

In some cases, our health is affected by the stress, frustration, irritation, etc. of our jobs. We know God, believe in God, but our job situation tends to dictate how we allow God's power to work in us. The best way to explain it is when we clock into work, we clock out of ministry! When we walk into the office, we leave God at the front door! When we walk into the office, we leave God at the security desk!

Some of us turn on our praise and worship in the car but turn it off, leaving it *and* God in the car when we get to work instead of walking into the "court" (the office) with the praise and worship! I can personally testify that on the days I allowed God to work in me, the days were peaceful despite the storm going on around me. But when I did not allow God to work in me, all hell broke loose! When the disciples were on the boat in rough seas, Jesus didn't take them out of the storm but calmed the storm. As a matter of fact, Jesus was resting below in the midst of the storm, which serves as a reminder to us that we can have peace in the midst of our storm (let that marinate).

When I think about Ephesians 3:20, I think about the power that flows from the pole to the box on our house. The power flows consistently to our house. Inside the house, we can choose to allow things to use that power. During the daytime, our lights may not shine because the switch is turned off, but the power is still running to the house. At night, our lights shine because we flip the switch and allow the power that consistently flows to our house to turn on the lights. God is our power source, and His power consistently flows to us. We determine if and when His consistent power will flow in us and through us (let that marinate)!

When you let the Power work in you, He will work for you! Jesus paid our power bill through His crucifixion and resurrection, so we don't have to conserve the Power like we do in our homes to maintain a low electricity bill. When you let the Power work in you, it will truly work in you and through you! When others see the Power working in you, they will be influenced to let the Power work in them, too! He is able to do exceedingly *abundantly* above all that we ask or think when we let His Power work in us! Let the Power work!

THE LORD IS ON YOUR SIDE

Psalm 118:5-6

The subject "The Lord is on Your Side" is a word all within itself! If you look back on your life, you *know* the Lord was on your side! He brought you out of some stuff that you just knew was going to bring your life to an end. He protected you from dangers seen and unseen. He delivered you from someone who didn't have your best interest at heart. For those of you still attached to that person who meant you no good, He *will* deliver you from them (let that marinate). In some situations, He delivered you from yourself (really let that marinate)! He brought you out of an "Egypt" situation and led you to your "promised land!" So, guess what? You are *still* here because the Lord is on your side!

It could've been you! It should've been you! It would've been you! But thanks to the Lord's grace and mercy, it wasn't you! When the enemy attacked you, His grace and mercy protected you! When you went through and continue to go through your storms, you don't look like what you have gone through or what you're going through because of His grace and mercy! When you were counted out, His grace and mercy counted you in! When man tried to put you down or keep you down, His grace and mercy lifted you up! When the doctor gave you a bad report, His grace and mercy showed up to deliver His report, and you are still here!

With the Lord on your side, you are blessed! With the Lord on your side, your needs will always be met! With the Lord on your side, the enemy can't stand against you! With the Lord on your side, man's ignorant intentions toward you will turn into stepping stones for you to your blessings (let that marinate)! With the Lord on your side, victory is yours! So, if you are going through something right now, be encouraged in knowing that the Lord is on your side. If He brought you out before, then He will bring you out again and again and again and again! Where do you stand? I don't know about you, but I am standing on the Lord's side!

No matter what it looks like, remember that the Lord is *always* on your side and always in control!

Related Reading

Psalm 56:9-11; Romans 8:31

YOUR BETTER DAYS ARE ON THE WAY

Psalm 30:5

From one survivor to another (yes, you are a survivor), today is the start of your better days! You are coming out of the storm! You are coming out of the rain! You are coming out of the sadness! You are coming out of the pain! *Today* is the start of your better days! Even though you may be standing in the midst of a storm, you are coming out of the storm! Even though the clouds hang over, the "Son" is piercing through and shining upon you; you are coming out of the rain!

Your strength will be renewed! Your peace will be restored! Your faith will be stronger than before! You will say bye-bye to fear and hello to joy! Your cup will overflow with new blessings! The things that bothered you before will not bother you anymore! The people that bothered you before will not bother you anymore! No more stressing! No more sleepless nights! No more heartaches! Your better days are on the way!

Yes, you have been in the storm for a long time, but guess what? You are *still* here!! The storm did not take you out! You didn't think you would make it, but God! God kept you even when you didn't want to be kept! God held on to you when you wanted to let go of Him! And through the grace of God, your better days are on the way! The storm lasts for a little while, but the joy of God lasts *forever!*

"Weeping may endure for a night, but joy comes in the morning! "

You've been through the fire, and you've been through the storm. You are a survivor! You didn't believe you would make it, but you did! The storm tossed you around, but it did not sink you! The pressure of your situation caused you to bend, but it did not break you! You were hard-pressed on every side but not crushed! You were struck down but not destroyed (2 Cor. 4:8).

The water was above your head, but you did not drown! You have been steadfast with immovable trust in God, and this is a reminder that your labor was and is not in vain! Today is the start of your better days, so speak it into the atmosphere, believe it, and rejoice in the Lord. You've passed the test, so your blessing is on the way: your better days!

Can you feel it coming? Can you see it coming? Walk into it! Step out to receive it! Open your mouth and speak it into the atmosphere! You got a new anointing! You got a new praise! You got a new mind! You got a new start! It is your time! It is your season! Hold your head up high and praise God because your better days are here!

Related Reading

1 Corinthians 15:58; Galatians 6:9

YOUR SEASON IS ON THE WAY

Haggai 2:6-9

My brothers and my sisters, your season is on the way! God is going to move on your situation in such a way that there will be a great shake up of things! There is going to be a great quake in your spirit, and you will be loosed from the hands of the enemy! He is going to shift some things and people around, restoring peace in your life! He is going to shift some people around to bless you! He is going to shift you to bless some people! Don't focus on stuff or people but keep your eyes on God, for He is going to send the rain to end your drought! He is going to send an abundance to bless you and the overflow to bless those who are connected to your life and willing to receive a blessing!

You may be tired but be encouraged! You may be ready to give up but keep going! His grace is *sufficient,* and when we are tired, He is strong! So wait on the Lord! As you wait on the Lord, pray! As you wait on the Lord, fast! As you wait on the Lord, meditate on His word! As you wait on the Lord, work in your purpose! As you wait, your spiritual muscles are strengthening! As you wait, He is rising up in you! As you wait, He is renewing your strength so you can continue to sow good seeds and reap a plentiful harvest!

In order to receive it, you have to believe it! And when you receive it, share your testimony with another to encourage them to hold on and wait for God. Weeping may endure for a night, but joy comes in the morning! Your morning is coming! Your joy is on the way! We walk by faith and not by sight; therefore, activate your faith, trust God, and let Him have His way!

This is your season! Whose season is it? This is *your* season! What season is it? This is your season of healing, your season of deliverance, your season of restoration, your season of financial increase, your season of *breakthrough!*

Hold on, my brothers! Hold on, my sisters! Your season is on the way!

Related Reading

Isaiah 40:30-31; Acts 16:26; Galatians 6:9

IN DUE SEASON

Galatians 6:9 – And let us not grow weary while doing good, for in due season we shall reap if we do not lose heart.

I think it would be an understatement to say that most of us have questioned when we will receive our blessings, especially when it seems as if everyone around us is receiving their blessings right now. It would be an understatement to say that we don't get frustrated waiting for our blessing. We become very impatient and try to complete some type of action that we feel will bring us closer to our blessing, but this actually delays us from receiving our blessing (let that marinate). I said years ago that we want to take the wheel from God in our impatient moments and head in the wrong direction. We want to control the ride instead of enjoying and embracing the chauffeured ride by God.

I would contend that there is a delay in receiving our blessing to see if we would truly trust God. When the children of Israel were brought out of Egypt, God led them by the way of the wilderness to see if any of them would change their mind and return to Egypt (read Exodus 13:17-18). Between the moment that the promise of a blessing is given and the moment that the blessing is received, there is a time of preparation for the blessing.

When a farmer plants a seed today, he does not expect full growth of the seed to occur over night. The farmer understands that the seed will require time, ongoing maintenance (watering, fertilizer, removing weeds...let that marinate), nurturing, and some hard work so that, when it is time, he can reap a good harvest!

In due season, you will receive your blessings! In due season, you will receive your breakthrough! In due season, you will receive your healing! In due season, you will receive a financial increase! In due season, you will receive your husband! In due season, you will receive your wife! In due season, your broken heart will be mended! In due season, all that you lost will be given back to you in abundance! In due season, you will reap providing you do not give up before the harvest comes!

Be encouraged! As the Scripture says, "be steadfast and immovable". Lean not on your own understanding but trust God with all your heart, and let Him direct your steps! It may not seem like it now, but everything you have gone through or what you are currently going through is for a reason. You *will* be blessed in due season!!

Related Reading

Ecclesiastes 3:1; 1 Corinthians 15:58; Proverbs 3:5-6

GIVE IT TO GOD AND REST

Psalm 55:22

My brothers and my sisters, whatever you are going through right now that may be stressing you, causing you to lose sleep, act out of character, etc. Declare, "*Today* is the day that my problem, my circumstance, my issue, my concerns, my stress, and my storm will be given to God." Humble yourself and lift your hands to God.

When you lift your hands to God, you take them off the very thing that is keeping you down! When you lift your hands to God, it is not a sign of weakness but an acknowledgment of the Almighty Power that rules over everything including your situation! When you lift your hands to God, you are surrendering so God can have His way! In return for letting go, He will renew your strength to keep pressing forward! In return for letting go, He will give you comfort in knowing that everything will work according to His will!

Worrying about your circumstances will not make them better. Stressing about your circumstances will not make them better. Losing sleep over your circumstances will not make them better. Oftentimes, we allow our circumstances to pull us away from what we know best, which is the Word of God.

So, if you are worrying, stressing, losing sleep, or enduring any other type of burden, let me remind you of His promise to you. In return for letting go, He will give you peace! It is His promise to give us peace in a time when we need peace. Matthew 11:28 says, "'Come to Me, all you who labor and are heavy laden, and I will give you rest.'" Don't take my word; taste and see for yourself!

There it is! The reminder you need to endure and get through your storm. Let go and give your circumstances to God! Let go and put your problems in the hands of the Father! Let go and watch God silence the winds of your storm! You best believe the enemy is not losing any rest as long as you show signs of weakness. Get the rest promised to you by God and put the works of the enemy to rest once and for all.

Give it to God and rest!

Related Reading

1 Peter 5:6-7

VICTORY BELONGS TO YOU

Psalm 3:8; Psalm 3:8 (NLT)

Beloved, the victory belongs to you! I know the victory belongs to you and me because it is given to us through Christ Jesus! Whatever you are going through, be encouraged in knowing that the victory belongs to you! The doctor has given you an unfavorable report. The victory belongs to Jesus! The stress of your job is getting to you. The victory belongs to Jesus! You have an unbearable pain in your body. The victory belongs to Jesus!

You are not sure where your next meal will come from, how you will pay your bills, or how you will provide for your family. The victory belongs to Jesus! No matter what you do, your husband or wife just doesn't want to act right. The victory belongs to Jesus! A loved one finds comfort in drugs and alcohol. The victory belongs to Jesus! People said you would never make it or never amount to anything. The victory belongs to Jesus!

Put your trust in Jesus! Put your hope in Jesus! Put your problem in the hands of Jesus! He will deliver you! He will pull you through! Whatever your circumstances, issue, or storm, the victory belongs to Jesus! Victory over financial debt belongs to Jesus! Victory over (any) addictions belongs to Jesus! Victory over people trying to bring you down belongs to Jesus! Victory over marital issues belongs to Jesus!

Victory over issues on your job belongs to Jesus! Victory over sickness belongs to Jesus! Victory over a broken heart belongs to Jesus! Death could not hold Jesus down, so your problems can't hold you down! The tomb could not contain Jesus, so your problems can't contain you! Jesus was victorious over death! Jesus was victorious over the tomb! The victory belongs to Jesus, and through Him, the victory belongs to *you!*

Related Reading

Genesis 50:20; 2 Chronicles 20:15; Romans 8:28, 31; 1 Corinthians 15:57

SURRENDER TO GOD

Job 11:13-15 (CEV) 1 Peter 5:7

Surrender to God! You continue to do things on your own and see no progress. Time to surrender! You continue to drive down roads leading to dead ends. Time to surrender! You continue to say things that make your situation worse than it was before you spoke your words. Time to surrender! Every time you get yourself in a hole, you look to Him to pull you out of the hole. Time to surrender! He has allowed you to go through what you have gone through and what you are going through because He trusts you and is waiting for you to trust Him. Time to surrender!

No matter what you decide to do, the road will always lead back to Him. Time to surrender! If you stumble and fall, He will pick you up (if you want to be picked up...let that marinate). Wait a minute! Could He have purposely placed you in your current position so you would surrender to Him? Could it be that He allowed you to carry the heavy burden so you would fall to your knees and surrender to Him?

Your surrendering is *not* a sign of weakness but an acknowledgement of God's power to intervene on your behalf! Your surrendering confirms your faith in the Word which says, "Casting all your care upon Him, for He cares for you." Your surrendering is not a sign of defeat but positions you to be victorious over your storm, victorious over your circumstances, victorious over your mess, victorious over your situation!

Don't continue to walk around with a heavy burden on your shoulder! Don't continue to toss and turn at night losing sleep over something or someone outside of your control! Don't continue to fight a battle that belongs to God (let that marinate)! Surrender it to God, and He will take care of you!

If you humble yourself in His sight, He will lift you up! He knows your heart and knows you want to do right, so turn to Him! Surrender your thoughts for His thoughts! Surrender your ways for His ways! Surrender your words for His words! Surrender your will for His will! Surrender your heart for His heart! Surrender to God!

Related Reading

Psalm 46:10

WILL YOU TRUST HIM?

Psalm 9:10

If you call on God and don't feel Him near you, will you trust Him? If God tells you to let go of things or people you feel that you have to hold on to, will you trust Him? If you walk into work and receive a pink slip for no reason at all, will you trust Him? If someone breaks your heart by turning on you, will you trust Him? If you have prayed and prayed and prayed but it seems like your prayers are going unanswered, will you trust Him?

If you lose things or people you hold so dearly, will you trust Him? When you feel that you are not being treated as you deserve, will you trust Him? When the doctors give you or a loved one an unfavorable report, will you trust Him? When He allows you to walk into the "lion's den" (work, school, home, etc.), will you trust Him? When He allows you to go through what you are going through, will you trust Him?

Will you trust Him only when you are going through something, or will you trust Him every day? Will you trust Him in your troubled times like you do when times are good? Will you trust Him when the world has turned its back to you? Will you trust Him when man crucifies you? Will you trust Him? Will you trust Him when your life is a living hell? Will you trust Him when odds are against you? Will you trust Him when things seem impossible? Will you trust Him? Can you trust Him when your (so-called) friends leave you in the dust? What if you call on Him but don't feel His presence, can you or will you trust and believe Him?

It's easy to say we believe in God but hard for us to show our trust in God. It's easy to say we trust God but hard for us to give our problems to God. Some may say, "Well, you don't understand my situation" or "You are not going through what I am going through." You are exactly right! I may not understand your situation or know what you are going through; however, I trust and believe that God understands and sees what you are going through. As a matter of fact, I believe when we are going through something, God is waiting for us to turn to Him so He can bring us out (let that marinate).

I don't know what you are going through at this very moment. I don't know the pain you are enduring. I don't know how many sleepless nights you've had. I don't know how tired you may be at this moment. I don't know the battle you are facing. I don't know the circumstance that is causing you to cry out to God. I don't know the weight that you are carrying that should be given over to God.

I don't know your situation, but I *do* know Who you can trust in your situation. I do know Who you should trust so you can rest at night! I do know Who you can trust so your strength can be restored! I do know Who you can trust in your battle which is not yours to fight in the first place (let that marinate)! I do know Who you can trust to keep you safe in the "lion's den"! I do know Who can give you peace in the middle of the storm!

Will you trust Him? The Lord is your Light and Salvation, so whom shall you fear? If God is your God, then trust in Him! If you know the name of God, then put your trust in Him! Psalm 84:12 says, "O Lord of hosts, Blessed is the man who trusts in You!" Trust Him!

Related Reading

Job 13:15a; Psalm 21:1; Psalm 31:14; Psalm 56:3-4

GOD'S GOT IT

The New International Version (NIV) of Exodus 14:14 says, "The Lord will fight for you; you need only to be still."

The New King James Version (NKJV) of Exodus 14:14 says, "The Lord will fight for you, and you shall hold your peace."

The English Standard Version (ESV) of Exodus 14:14 says, "The Lord will fight for you, and you have only to be silent."

The New Living Translation (NLT) of Exodus 14:14 says, "The Lord Himself will fight for you. Just stay calm."

The Message version (MSG) of Exodus 14:14 says, "God will fight the battle for you. And you? You keep your mouths shut!"

For a few weeks, the Holy Spirit has taken me back to thoughts given to me within the last few years. How many of you know that the Blood never loses its power? The Word of God never loses its power! The grass withers, the flower fades, but the Word of our God stands forever! After you have done all you can, stand on the Word that is strong! Stand on the Word that is mighty! Stand on the Word that will never let you down! Stand on the Word that will fight your battles for you!

It's amazing how you can read multiple versions of the same Scripture and receive different yet explicit direction, guidance, revelation, etc. For those of you in the midst of a battle, here is the word for you to stand on:

Be still, hold your peace, be silent, stay calm, and keep your mouth shut because God will fight the battle for you!

WILL YOU GO THROUGH TO GET YOUR BREAKTHROUGH?

Mark 2:2-5, 11-12

Will you go through to get to your breakthrough? Our faith should drive us to get through whatever it is we are going through. Though there were many surrounding Jesus, the men did not allow the rest of the crowd to stop them from getting their friend to Jesus so he could be healed. In this context, I see the four men as friends of the paralytic man because true friends will be with you no matter what and will do whatever they can to help you (let that marinate).

They came with a purpose and did not allow the circumstances stop that purpose! They lifted the paralytic man up, broke through the roof, and lowered him down. Can I help you? Your breakthrough comes with the lifting of your hands to God in praise and the lowering of yourself to your knees in prayer and worship!

The paralytic man is a significant person in this account as we can relate to him. We allow our storms, our situations, our circumstances to paralyze us all because of what they look like and allow them to hinder us from achieving our breakthrough. We can be on the edge of our breakthrough but be afraid to keep going to receive it. We can be one step away from our breakthrough but be afraid to take that final step into our breakthrough. Oh, and sometimes, we let our pride get in the way which pushes those away who really have our best interest at heart and want to help us get our breakthrough! God will send us the help we need in the time of need through a vessel or vessels of His choice. Don't be so quick to turn away the help sent to help your breakthrough (let that marinate, too).

And when you achieve your breakthrough, share your testimony! Your breakthrough is not just for you but for others going through! Do not be ashamed of what you are going through or what you have been through. If you are ashamed of what you have been through before the breakthrough, then are you ashamed to talk about the One who gave you the breakthrough (my God, let that marinate).

When the man arose from his paralytic state, the witnesses were amazed and said, "We never saw anything like this!" When you get your breakthrough, others should be in awe and know that if God did it for you, He will do it for them, too! When you get your breakthrough, it should bring hope to others who may be going through the same thing as you! When you get your breakthrough, it should encourage others to keep pushing to achieve their breakthrough! When you get your breakthrough, it should glorify the magnificent works of God! Your breakthrough is on the way!

You *will* go through and get your breakthrough!

THE ROAD WILL GET BETTER

The road we travel is not easy. We will have some good days and endure some bad days. We will have some days that will make us smile and some days that will make us cry. We will have some calm days and some stormy days. We've had some days in which we didn't think we would see another day. You may have or have had days on which you were questioning why you were going through what you were going through.

You may have asked, "Lord, why me?" You may be asking, "What did I do to deserve this?" You may feel that, though you are doing things right, things are going wrong. Well, there is a word for you on this day. You may be tired but keep pressing! You may feel that your labor is in vain, but it's not! You may feel that all is lost, but joy is on the way!

And let us not grow weary while doing good, for in due season we shall reap if we do not lose heart (Galatians 6:9).

But thanks be to God, who gives us the victory through our Lord Jesus Christ. Therefore, my beloved brethren, be steadfast, immovable, always abounding in the work of the Lord, knowing that your labor is not in vain in the Lord.

(1 Corinthians 15:57-58).

My brethren, count it all joy when you fall into various trials, knowing that the testing of your faith produces patience (James 1:2).

Don't allow your circumstances to consume you! Don't allow your circumstances to discourage you! Don't allow your circumstances to ruin your harvest! Don't allow the pain you are feeling to discourage you from pressing toward your blessing! Don't walk away from the storm but lift up your head and walk through the storm!

You have planted good seeds in fertile soil, and you shall reap what you sow! Every situation will only make you stronger, so stay strong my brothers and sisters! You can't stop now! You can't give up! It may be dark, but light is coming! It may be midnight, but your morning is on the way! You may be going through, but you are coming out! You may be weeping, but joy is on the way. Don't lose heart! Count it all joy; it *will* get better. No matter the weapon, it will not and shall not prosper!

The road you are on now may not be easy, but it *will* get better!

PEACE IN THE STORM

Mark 4:37-41

In the midst of trouble, the disciples were worried and panicking because it appeared that they were in danger. Jesus was asleep below in the stern of the boat. As many times as I have read this account, it really hit me that Jesus was asleep in the storm, which is a good reminder that we, too, can rest in our storm (let that marinate). The disciples called to Jesus and asked if He did not care about their situation.

If you think about it, Jesus could have calmed the storm at any time, and one would think He knew they were in the storm but did not move. Could it be that He waits to see how we will respond before displaying His power? Could it be that He wants to see the level of our faith before jumping into action? Something to think about indeed; let it marinate!

No matter your storm, whether it is work, home, family, school, depression, anxiety, stress, finances, etc., there is peace! When the winds of trouble start to stir up, stir up your faith! When the rain starts to fall, open your faith to shield you! When the clouds roll in, look to the "Son" to light a path for you! Don't be surprised if Jesus doesn't calm your storm but calms you to help you get through the storm (let that marinate).

When you are in a storm, remind yourself that Peace is always in the storm with you and your Peace is Jesus!

I AM THE PROBLEM

Jonah 1:10-16

In the account of Jonah, we know that God gave him an assignment and he chose to run from that assignment. Jonah went to Joppa and found a ship going to Tarshish. He paid his fare and boarded the ship. Because he was on the *wrong* ship (let that marinate), God sent a great wind that disturbed the sea. The "innocent" crew was afraid, and when the captain approached Jonah, Jonah revealed his identity. When the crew asked Jonah what they should do, he told them to throw him overboard. When they threw him overboard, the winds ceased, and the sea was calm. Jonah knew he was the cause of the great wind and sea disturbance. He was the problem!

How many times have you been on the "wrong ship" and wondered why you were dealing with rough seas? How many times have you blamed someone else for the storm you were enduring? How many times have you thrown someone off the "ship" and *still* endured rough seas (really let that marinate)? Jonah took accountability for the trouble the ship crew was enduring at sea. It takes a real person (man or woman) to admit his or her wrongs. It takes a real person to take responsibility for his or her actions. Some may see it as a sign of weakness, but it takes strength and courage to say "I'm wrong" or hold yourself responsible for your actions.

If you are enduring the same thing with different people, you are the problem and not the people. You tend to think the variable numerator is the cause of our problems when, in actuality, you are the common denominator and root of your problems. I love the tag line from one of my favorite childhood cartoons, G.I. Joe: "Knowing is half the battle."

When you know that you are the problem, half the battle is won! When you know that you are the problem, you move closer to the solution for the problem. When you know that you are the problem, you are opening the door to be put in a position to fix yourself. When Jonah was thrown overboard, he was swallowed by the great fish, and for three days, God dealt with him. When you know that you are the problem, then you are in the right position for God to deal with you (let that marinate).

When your ship is being rocked, don't blame others for the turbulence you are experiencing. When things are not going right, don't blame others because things are not going right. Others can't make you do what you don't want to do. The enemy can't make you do anything. It is you who decides to do what you decide to do. Others are not the problem. You are the problem. Be bold enough to admit "I am the problem" so the winds of trouble can cease from blowing and you can sail in peaceful seas.

FRESH BREAD

Matthew 4:4 (NIV)

Too many of us are living off old bread. We are allowing the taste of bread received last week, last month, last year, or years ago to sustain us in our present situation. When you purchase a fresh loaf of bread, it is pleasing to the eye, nose, tongue and stomach. After a few days, it may still look, smell, and taste good, and it may fill your stomach. If the conditions are not favorable to sustain the bread, it will start looking less appealing, developing a smell, and tasting bad. Then, your stomach may not receive it.

Eventually, we discard the old bread for some new bread. Can I help you with something? We have some old bread to discard because it is not sustaining us anymore. We've taken bread that blessed us in one season into another season, and it has now transformed into a burden. Yes, a burden. It is a burden because it is blocking you from receiving new bread. It's blocking you like security blocking wild fans at a concert. It's blocking you like the offensive line of a football team protecting their quarterback.

We put on fresh under garments everyday (or I pray that you do). We get fresh every morning in preparation for work, school, etc. by taking a shower, brushing our teeth, fixing our hair, and putting on fresh clothes. Lord knows we get fresh for worship on Sundays and super fresh for Easter, Mother's Day, and Christmas services. We can get fresh in various aspects of our lives but stay content with being stale in the Word.

"Give us *this* day our daily bread" (Matt. 6:11). If you believe those words that you say in your prayer, then don't settle on stale bread and, instead, receive the fresh bread He has for you!

SEED OF INSPIRATION

A seed placed in the right conditions will achieve a breakthrough. The seed is placed in fertile soil, the right soil for it. The seed is fed nutrients so it can grow. The seed grows in the darkness of the soil, and what we see on top is the result of the seed's strength, perseverance, growth, maturity, etc. But even after the seed has achieved its breakthrough, the flower that blossoms still needs the right nutrients, "light," and care so life can be sustained. There is life after the breakthrough.

There is a "seed" who feels he or she may not achieve a breakthrough. Sometimes, the confirmation you need may come in the form of a simple yet strong analogy; this is a bold confirmation that your breakthrough is coming. You are in darkness, one of the right conditions for a seed to achieve a breakthrough. In darkness, you are being fed the "nutrients" (prayer, meditation, study of the Word, etc.) necessary to help you achieve your breakthrough. I believe that sometimes He has to put us in a place so we will stop doing and His will can start working in us. You haven't given up because you are more than a conqueror and you believe it!. Yes, you have experienced some tiresome moments, but the Holy Spirit brings to your remembrance the following:

> *And let us not grow weary while doing good, for in due season we shall reap if we do not lose heart (Galatians 6:9)*

> *He gives power to the weak, And to those who have no might He increases strength. Even the youths shall faint and be weary, And the young men shall utterly fall, But those who wait on the Lord Shall renew their strength; They shall mount up with wings like eagles, They shall run and not be weary, They shall walk and not faint (Isaiah 40:29-31)*

When you receive your breakthrough, the result will be a representation of God's glory! It won't be about you but what God did for you! It will be about how He brought you out of the darkness into the light. Don't stop with the breakthrough because there is life after the breakthrough! You must sustain your breakthrough with continuous prayer, meditation, study, etc., all the things you did in the darkness. Most flowers need an adequate supply of sunlight, so make sure you get your daily dose of the "Son" to help sustain your life. You will be a flower that stands in awe of God's greatness, God's power, God's glory and be an inspiration, motivation, and confirmation for other "seeds" to achieve their breakthroughs.

It is your season for a breakthrough, and it is coming for you!

LESSON FROM FACEBOOK UNFOLLOW AND FOLLOW

Matthew 4:18-20

This thought is not one to make you shout or make you dance. Sometimes, we need a word that pierces our souls or makes us examine ourselves. We all have some things or people in our lives, not necessarily bad, whose presence is keeping us from Jesus. Jesus sacrificially gave His life for *our* salvation. What will you sacrifice to follow Him? Who will you "unfriend" to follow Him? What mess (yes, I said it) will you "unfollow" to follow the risen Savior? What dead situation in your life will you finally lay to rest so you can live in Christ Jesus?

As I was looking at the various options and settings on Facebook, the following came to mind (if you are a Facebook user, then you can really relate to this).

If you hide or unsubscribe from a friend, his or her updates do not appear in your news feed. However, this friend's words are still accessible if you go to his or her page. If you "unfriend" someone, he or she will no longer appear on your friend's list, and there is a possibility that you can still view this person's page depending upon his or her account/privacy settings. Access is still present.

If you block someone, he or she will be gone completely, including access to his or her page. If you frequent the social network sites, then I am quite sure you have either used the "unfriend" option on Facebook so you can no longer see negativity in your news feed or used the "unfollow" option on Twitter or Instagram so that you don't receive annoying tweets or view tasteless pictures.

Can I help you out with something? Some of us are simply hiding from our mess (people, situation, things, etc.) and still have access to the mess. Some of us try to "unfriend" our mess but leave the door open (access) for the mess to return. You need to block the mess so that it is gone completely and can no longer have access to you.

Treat your mess like you treat some unwanted people on Facebook. Block your mess so it (or they) can't mess with you. Only messy people like to keep up with a mess, and surely, you are not a messy person. Let it go! Unfollow and follow Him!

Related Reading

Matthew 8:21-22; Matthew 9:9

NO BOUNDARIES

1 Chronicles 4:9-10

The two verses about Jabez are powerful as he did not limit himself to the boundaries of his namesake placed upon him by his mother. It is a great example of how we do not have to accept things or circumstances as they are. It is a great example of how we should make our requests known to God, which is scriptural. Philippians 4:6 says, "Be anxious for nothing, but in everything by prayer and supplication, with thanksgiving, let your requests be known to God."

Let's be honest, many of us have become comfortable in our situations, accepting things as they are. We want to stay in the comfort zone because of the comfort we think resides inside of our own make-shift boundaries. We don't want to change or endure change. We don't want to step out into something we can't see. We don't want to have to start over. We simply make excuses for our unwillingness to step outside the boundaries set in our minds. It's time to take the limits off! Jabez removed the boundaries of his name through a simple yet powerful prayer to God. Not only did God hear his request but fulfilled it! Same God! If He did it before, He will do it again!

God has much more for you than what you have experienced or witnessed thus far. Yes, He has blessed you in this or past seasons, but don't get caught up in those seasons when He has many more seasonal blessings lined up for you. Don't become complacent or stagnant in your right now when your future is much greater! Jabez took charge and changed his situation. He stepped beyond the boundaries and was even smart enough to ask God to enlarge his territory.

If you think it, God can do it. "Now to Him who is able to do exceedingly abundantly above all that we ask or think, according to the power that works in us" (Eph. 3:20). No boundaries! Take the limits off and be released into what God has for you! I see you in the future, and you look much better than you do right now!

LET HIM PREPARE YOU

After buying a pack of meat, most people will take it home for either future or immediate use. Most people I know do not take the meat out of the package, place it in a cooking container, and then commence cooking it without adding to it. Unless you have a highly different sense of taste or a medical need, who likes to eat bland meat? Not me.

Most people I know generally take the meat out of the package and prep it. Depending on the meat, it may be thoroughly washed first. Next, it is seasoned to fit a specific taste. While the meat is being prepared, the oven is being pre-heated so that it is ready when the meat is ready. Once the prepping is done, the meat is placed in or on the stove depending on if it is being fried or baked. During the cooking process, the meat is periodically checked to ensure it is cooked thoroughly.

If it is taken out too early, then it is not edible and could actually cause sickness. If it is taken out too late, then it may not be edible or as fulfilling. When the time is right, the meat is removed from the oven and served. Each morsel melts in your mouth as the seasonings enhance the flavor of the meat. The nutrients fulfill the needs of your body as the meat is consumed. You are blessed by the meat that was prepped, seasoned, and cooked just right. Oh, taste and see!

I contend that God can bless us any time He desires but chooses the right time, the time when we are ready to receive the blessing. See,

He unpacks us and prepare us for the blessing. He washes the impurities away so that we don't ruin the blessing. After He washes us, He seasons us with grace and mercy. Grace and mercy protect us from the next step, the fire.

Oh, blessings do not come easy. It takes us going through something to get to the blessing. It is grace and mercy that help us to come out of the fire with no scars. We don't look like what we've been through thanks to grace and mercy! The fire burns off anything we may have acquired after being washed by the blood! The fire reminds us that God is in control and what we will receive is *not* from our actions but God's will.

God allows us to go to the fire, through the fire, and He brings us out of the fire at the right time. After the fire, we receive the blessing. Through it all, we have to trust the Master Chef. When you trust Him, you will be blessed! Psalm 34:8 says *"Oh, taste and see that the Lord is good; blessed is the man who trusts Him!"* God has prepared your blessings, so let Him prepare you to receive them!

MAKE PEACE WITH YOUR PAST

Philippians 3:13-14

In life, we endure sunny, cloudy, and rainy days. We have our moments of conquering great feats and other moments in which we may feel defeated. We smile brightly at our achievements and hold our heads low at our disappointments. We are quick to share the highlights of life and quick to hide the shadow-casting moments of life. For some of us, we tackle life's obstacles and keep it moving. Unfortunately, most find themselves at a standstill, wallowing in the mud of despair, unable to move forward because they are stuck in their pasts. You messed up. So what!? You made a mistake. So what!?

We can't walk into our futures because we are focused on our pasts. If you allow your past to interfere with your present, then there is no future. I coined that phrase as a reminder to press forward, not backward. For many of us, we are walking backward because we haven't let go of our pasts. It is time to sprinkle some present rain on the past dust so it can settle.

Things come to an end for a reason, so let it end. In everything we do, there are lessons to be learned. Learn your lesson and keep moving. Until you make peace with your past, your present peace will be a mere thought and not a reality. So make peace with your past today so you can enjoy the blessings of the present and position yourself to receive the blessings of the future.

Please join me in prayer:

"Father God, thank You for bringing us this far. There were times when we couldn't see our way through, but by Your grace, Your mercy, Your strength, we are still here. And because we are still here, we say thank You. Thank You for keeping us when we didn't want to be kept. Thank You for forgiving and forgetting our ways. Thank You for being the loving Father You are to us at all times.

"Lord, help us to forgive ourselves. Help us to forget those things that we did that were not of Your will. Remind us that when You forgive and forget, we should forgive and forget, too. Now, Lord, remove those past thoughts that keep us from doing Your will. Remove those past obstacles, man and things, that keep us from doing Your will. Guide us, protect us, strengthen us, consume us, comfort us, and love us as we walk in Your good and perfect will! These and other blessings we ask in Your Son Jesus's name. Amen!"

Related Reading

Ecclesiastes 7:8; Isaiah 43:18

WHEN YOU NEED A WORD

2 Timothy 3:16

I think we all enter a moment or period in which we need a word from God. If you are like me, you need a word every day and not just on the days you are going through something. Sometimes, we allow the noise pollution of life to dampen our hearing and rely on a "Miracle Ear" to amplify the word from God so we can hear and receive it. Sometimes, we wait until Sunday morning to receive a much-needed word and forget that God speaks Monday through Saturday (let that marinate). When I need a word, I've found that the following formula works for me:

•Find a quiet, relaxing place to pray. Ask God to open your mind, heart, spirit, and understanding to receive His word.

•Open your Bible. The word you seek will be found in the Scripture.

•Take your time. Do not force the word but allow it to come to you.

•Reflect and meditate on the Scripture(s) you read. As I love to say, let it marinate!

•Write out your thoughts. Habakkuk 2:2 says, "Then the Lord answered me and said: 'Write the vision and make it plain on tablets, that he may run who reads it.'" Sometimes, when you write your thoughts after reading the Bible, they become plain to you and reveal the word you were seeking.

•Share your thoughts. It is amazing that, when I share my thoughts, the Holy Spirit continues to work with the ingredients in my spirit and cooks up an on-time word.

By no means would I imply that the aforementioned formula is the best in receiving a word from God, but I am offering the formula to you as a starting point when you need a word. One of our problems is that we don't like to share our blessings with others so we can all experience the blessings God has for us. I pray my sharing is a blessing to someone and I can give Him praise for blessing me to be a blessing!

147

Just remember that if you are blessed, be a blessing to someone else; pay it forward!

If you need a word, I pray not only that God gives you the word you seek, but I also pray you hear and receive the word!

SEEK UNDERSTANDING

Luke 24:45

As I was meditating on the word preached at a revival service, the following thought was birthed: Anyone can quote Scriptures, but not everyone can or will unlock the power of the Scriptures. When you embrace the words you speak, they become a formidable weapon to use against the enemy."

Undoubtedly, there *is* power in the Word. We miss opportunities to call upon the power due to our lack of understanding of the power in the Word. The Word even tells us that "death and life are in the power of the tongue" (Prov. 18:21). I would contend that the words we speak have power but we lack the knowledge of the power.

In Jesus's final appearance to the disciples as captured by Luke, the Word is significant and applicable to us today. In fact, I would contend that it should be part of our daily prayer: "Lord, open my understanding so I may comprehend the Scripture." A very familiar quote, "Knowledge is Power," is true. It's so true that I am convinced that one of Satan's reasons for attacking God's children is so we will remain in a state of misunderstanding, which prevents us from utilizing the power of God given by God when He made us in the likeness of His image. When you don't know, Satan is pleased. However, when you know the Word, Satan knows he is in trouble because he can't stand against the Word of God.

Don't be satisfied with quoting the Word. Don't be satisfied with being able to recognize the Word. Seek a true understanding of the Word and let the Word work for you.

STEP OUT OF YOUR BOAT

Matthew 14:25-32

How many times have you faced a decision and been afraid to decide because you were not sure of its outcome? How many times have you had an opportunity to walk into something, decided not to walk into it, and realized afterward that you should have walked into the opportunity that presented itself to you? How many times have you talked yourself out of doing something because you weren't sure where it was going to lead or if it was right for you? How many of you are simply afraid to step outside your comfort zone, step outside of the box?

Oftentimes, we are presented with an opportunity to step out of our "boat" but are afraid because we don't know what would happen if we made that step. Oftentimes, we are afraid to step out of our "boat" because we don't want to change or fear change. On the flip side, some of us take a few steps away from our "boat" but turn around to get back in it because things don't appear as we desire them to appear.

When Jesus commanded Peter to come out to Him, to step out of the boat, Peter asked Him to confirm His identity. At first, Peter stepped out boldly upon the water to walk toward Jesus. But alas, the wind raised fear in him, and he began to sink. Let me stop right there. What is the "wind" (finances, relationships, family, friends, enemies, etc.) in your life that is causing you to be afraid to step boldly out of your "boat"? What is the "wind" in your life that is distracting you from your focus on Jesus? Let's be real. We *all* have some type of "wind" that has caused us to fear leaving the comfort of our "boat." Here is the good news. Even when you step out and start to sink, all you have to do is call on the name of Jesus; He will save you.

Don't let your thoughts of the unknown keep you from stepping out of your "boat." The Word tells us in Proverbs (3:5-6) that we should trust in the Lord and lean *not* on our (what?) own understanding. If we proclaim faith, our actions should support our proclamation. Yes, stepping out of your "boat" will be stepping out into the unknown; that's faith.

149

And be not afraid of what you are stepping into if your steps are ordered by God. When we step out on the path God made for us, there is no need to be afraid because He knows the outcome. He knows what we are walking into. He knows what we will do before we will do it and has it worked out already for us.

With the light of God on your side, fear should not exist. With the strength of God in your life, fear can be conquered. With the presence of God in your life, fear should flee from you. If God commands you to step out of your "boat," step out on faith. Step out trusting Him. Step out with your eyes focused on Him. Don't be distracted by the "winds" of the world. And if by chance you start sinking, just call on His name, and He will raise you so you can continue your journey. Don't wait any longer. Step out of your "boat"!

Related Reading

Psalm 27:1; Hebrews 11:1

RELEASE YOUR ANCHOR

Matthew 11:28-30

If you look up the word "anchor," it may be defined as a heavy object attached to a vessel by a cable, rope, or chain and dropped into the water to keep the vessel in place either by its weight or by its flukes, which grip the bottom. When a ship is docked, the anchor is lowered to keep it from drifting away. When the ship is ready to go to sea, the anchor is drawn so it can move. The physical use of the anchor works differently in the spiritual realm.

Whereas the physical anchor keeps a ship from moving, we have some spiritual anchors that need to be released so *we* can move! Your "anchor" may be depression, stress, a broken heart, mistrust, failed relationships, disappointments, feelings of inadequacies, or low self-esteem; whatever you may be dealing with that's keeping you *down* is your "anchor"! You can't walk into your destiny because your "anchor" is holding you back! It's taking you a long time to reach your blessing because of the "anchor" you are dragging! You are not moving because your "anchor" has brought you to a complete stop!

Today is the day that you release your "anchor." You are not resting because of your "anchor." Your health is being attacked because of your "anchor." People are catching hell from you because of your "anchor" (let that marinate). You are blaming everyone except yourself because *your* "anchor" is holding you still!

You release your "anchor," and Jesus will give you rest! Release your "anchor" and start moving again! Release your "anchor" because it is too heavy for you to bear but just right for Jesus to carry! Release your "anchor" to The Anchor! Simply put, "anchor" can also be defined as a support! *Jesus* is our Anchor! When we anchor ourselves in Him, nothing can stop us from moving! *Nothing* can hold us down!

"No weapon formed against you [or me] shall prosper!" Our "anchors" will not prosper! Our "anchors" will not hold us down any longer! Declare and decree today that your "anchor" will be released! Give it to Jesus! Let it go so you can go! Release your "anchor"!

Related Reading

1 Peter 5:6-7

AFTER THE SERVICE

Matthew 28:16-17; Mark 16:15-20; Luke 24:50-53

The Scriptures above give us three separate accounts of Jesus's ascension to heaven. The disciples worshiped, Jesus gave them a word, He ascended to heaven, and the disciples departed the place to carry the received instructions. As I was reading the accounts, I thought about Sunday worship. On Sunday morning, we go to a place appointed for us, our respective churches. Most worship services open with praise and worship or a devotion which sets the atmosphere to receive the Word that is to be preached on that given day.

Skipping over traditional preliminaries (announcements, offerings, scriptural readings, choir singing, etc.), the man or woman of God brings forth the word to His people. The word may be convicting, thought-provoking, comforting, healing, a release, or an opportunity to celebrate the God we serve. The temperature of the spirits in the house may depend upon the word being preached and how it is received by the hearers of the word.

The temperature may be high, leading to more praise and worship, people speaking in tongues, people laid out at the altar, etc. The temperature may be lukewarm, resulting in a few surrendering their life to Christ or a "pity-pat" praise showing acceptance of the word. We won't touch upon a cold temperature of the spirits in the house as it's a matter of its own. After the word has been preached and the benediction delivered, we depart from the house of God to our respective houses. When praise and worship is over and the energy of the word is no more, then what? What do you do "after the service"?

When Jesus gave the disciples final instructions or words, they departed from that place and went out to preach the gospel. Based upon the accounts, they did not get caught up in the euphoria of praise and worship. What do I mean? We (including me) can get caught up in the euphoria of praise and worship and turn it off as soon as we set one foot out of the church doors. The disciples continued to praise and bless the name of God even after Jesus left them. They went out to preach the gospel that was given to them. After the service, they continued to work.

So what are you doing after the service? Are you praising and worshipping Him but returning to those things that do not magnify Him? After the service, does your praise continue, or does it cut off when someone cuts you off on your way home? After the service, are you speaking a "tongue" different from the one spoken during worship? If you were looking for a feel-good word, let me apologize to you now, for this is not it.

This is a self-examination or convicting word. This is a word to encourage you and me to continue our praise, our worship after the service has ended. This is a word to remind you and me that we are His vessels and we should carry the word we receive out to the world. There is more to the worship experience in the house. There is work to be done "after the service."

DELAYED WITH A PURPOSE

Exodus 13:17-18

How many times you were frustrated because of some type of delay? How many times have you been upset because something you expected or wanted to occur did not occur within the timeframes of *your* mind? How many times have you given up on something or someone because the result you desired was delayed in coming to you?

Let's be honest. At some point in our lives, we have become disappointed, upset, stressed, angry, etc. due to some type of delay whether it be traffic, an unexpected change of weather, or waiting for the promise to come to fruition versus a promise from God now (let that marinate). There were times I wanted to leave home at a certain time, experienced a delay, and passed an accident on the same route I was taking. Of course, I prayed for those involved in the accident and thanked God that I was delayed because it could have been me.

Though we don't understand or see it at the time, there is a *reason* for the delays that occur in our lives. A delay can test our free will. God could have easily guided the children of Israel into the promised land; however, He took them a different, longer route in case they decided to change their minds and go back to Egypt. Our delayed moment tests us to see if we will go back to our "Egypt" or if we will lean not on our own understanding, trust Him, and keep going forward.

A delay is merely preparation for our blessing. It is ironic that sometimes, during our moments of delay, we experience difficult times or obstacles. These times test our spirits, faith, and trust in God. We experience some pruning, cutting, releasing, and a spiritual surgery during these times, all of which are necessary to build us up, strengthen us, or position us to receive the promises of God. I would contend that He will not bless us if we are not ready to receive it. The delay prepares us for our blessing.

Last but not least, a delay tests your heart and trust in God. Are you after God for Him or the stuff He can give you? Are you after God to be used by Him or to use Him for your own gain (let that marinate)? A delay tests your heart and trust. The delay is like the thorn in our side as eloquently described by Paul in 2 Corinthians 12:7-10. The delay reminds us that His grace is sufficient and His strength will be made perfect through our weaknesses. We are allowed to experience delays so that our hearts are humbled and reminded that God is God. If He brought us this far, He will continue to carry us. If we humble ourselves in the sight of God during our delayed moments, He will lift us up out of those moments!

Your delay is for a reason. The job you desire is delayed for a reason. The husband or wife you desire is delayed for a reason. The financial blessing you seek is delayed for a reason. There is a reason for the delay. There is a purpose for your delay. So, during the delay, do not lose heart! Wait patiently for Him, trust in Him! His word will not return to Him void as it will accomplish and prosper in the very thing for which He sent it. You may be a step away from your blessing. Don't let your delay turn you around now. What God has for you is coming; wait for it!

Related Reading

Deuteronomy 8:2; Psalm 37:5-7

EMBRACE YOUR DELAY

Habakkuk 2:3 (NLT)

When you are engaged in your personal study of the Word, it is sometimes helpful to reference multiple translations of the Word to gain an understanding of it. Have you noticed how God will give us a vision, a plan, a promise, or a purpose but won't give us a time as to when His word would be fulfilled? We receive His word, and then we enter a period dreaded by most, the waiting period. Let's be real; most of us do not like to wait on people or things. When we want something, we want it right then and there and don't care what it takes to get it. We just want it. Because we want what we want at that given moment, we accept people or things who are not meant for us (let that marinate).

When we accept people or things who are not meant for us, it takes a period of time to undo our mess and get us ready for what He has for us. We see this period between the announcement of the promise, our impatience, getting back on track to the promise, and the fulfillment of the promise as a delay. It is during our "delay" that we embrace the spirit of doubt and question whether or not we will receive God's promise. It is during our "delay" that we question why it is taking so long to receive what God promised.

He promised financial blessing, but you have been living from paycheck to paycheck for the last ten years. In the last ten years, you haven't been tithing (which is not about the money but your faithfulness to give back to Him) and wonder why the promise has yet to be fulfilled. He promised you a husband or wife, yet you continue to give spousal benefits to those who were not ordained to be your spouse (let that marinate, too). He promised you a professional position that would be a blessing to you and those connected to you; however, you can't humble yourself long enough to appreciate or be content in your current position.

We could go on and on through multiple examples, but the point is what you see as a "delay" is necessary to undo those things that cannot be carried over into a new blessing. The children of Israel were delivered from Egypt and experienced a "delay" in the wilderness. They complained about being in the wilderness, and God heard their complaints but still provided. I would contend that the delay in the wilderness was intentional or part of the plan to get the children out of Egypt and to get Egypt out of the children (another marinate moment).

2 Peter 3:9 says, "The Lord is not slack concerning His promise, as some count slackness, but is long suffering toward us, not willing that any

should perish but that all should come to repentance." Psalm 27:14 says, "Wait on the Lord; Be of good courage, And He shall strengthen your heart; Wait, I say, on the Lord!" Isaiah 55:11 says, "'So shall My word be that goes forth from My mouth; It shall not return to Me void, But it shall accomplish what I please, And it shall prosper in the thing for which I sent it.'"

God will do exactly what He said He will do. As we wait on Him, we have to show our faithfulness to Him through our actions (prayer, study, fasting, meditation, treatment of one another, etc.). As we wait on Him, we should go to Him, repent for our wrongdoings, and get ourselves ready for the fulfillment of His promise. The waiting period or "delay" is for our good so embrace it. Allow God to have His way with you as you wait so you can not only be prepared to receive your blessing or appreciate your blessing but give Him your best praise, your best worship regardless of the blessing!

CHECK YOUR FOUNDATION

Matthew 16:18

Every house or building has a foundation. Construction of a new structure begins with a foundation on good soil that can support the foundation and structure. In my lifetime, I have yet to see a house or building built from the top down. It is built from the bottom up. From time to time, one should check the house inside and outside for any noticeable shift or cracks in the structure. The changes may indicate a problem with the foundation and a specialist may have to be called in to repair or strengthen the foundation! If you allow the foundational problems to persist, your house may not continue to stand and may eventually fall. Your house is only as good as its foundation!

"What does this have to do with me?" I'm glad you asked. Check your foundation! What is your foundation? God is your foundation! Jesus is your foundation! The Word of God is your foundation! Have you ever wondered how someone can still smile when all hell is breaking loose in his life? Check his foundation! Have you ever wondered how someone is able to worship God when she experiences the loss of a loved one? Check her foundation! Have you ever wondered how someone can still smile after receiving a pink slip from work? Check his or her foundation!

There is a quote by Gordon B. Hinckley that says, "You can't build a great building on a weak foundation. You must have a solid foundation if you're going to have a strong superstructure." The things we endure can make us go crazy, stress us out, or cause us to inflict harm on ourselves if our foundation is weak! We will come crashing down if our foundation is weak. Our "superstructure" will not stand if our foundation is weak! If you are weak in the Word, then you make it easy for the enemy to disrupt your house.

The enemy comes to kill, steal, and destroy. If your foundation is weak, then you make it easy for him to destroy your house with his wrecking ball! If you are constantly going through stuff and wondering why you are an easy target for the enemy, check your foundation! If it feels like things are falling apart in your life; check your foundation! If you are having problems on your job, then check your foundation! If you are having issues with your children, check *your* foundation and *their* foundations!

It is my belief (right or wrong) that when Jesus said in Matthew 16:18, "On this rock I will build My church," the rock represents the Word (foundation), while the Church is us. If you build the Church on the Word, the enemy can't prevail. If we build ourselves on the foundation of the Word, no devil in hell can be victorious over us! Two of the little pigs from the famous children's story were not wise in how they built their houses, and the wolf prevailed against both of them. They didn't have a strong foundation for their houses. The third little pig built a strong house, a strong tower on a strong foundation that spoiled the wolf's attack. Too many of us have houses like the two little pigs and not enough have a strong house like the third little pig (let that marinate).

Don't be ignorant to Satan's attempts to weaken your foundation and bring down your house. He may huff, he may puff, but he won't be able to bring down your house if your foundation is strong! Your foundation is the Word of God! Your foundation is Jesus! You won't be able to stand if your foundation cannot support your standing (let that marinate).

Check your foundation!

Related Reading

Proverbs 18:10; 1 Corinthians 15:58; Ephesians 6:13

FROM GOOD TO GREAT

And Peter answered Him and said, "Lord, if it is You, command me to come to You on the water." So He said, "Come." And when Peter had come down out of the boat, he walked on the water to go to Jesus. But when he saw that the wind was boisterous, he was afraid; and beginning to sink he cried out, saying, "Lord, save me!" And immediately Jesus stretched out His hand and caught him, and said to him, "O you of little faith, why did you doubt?" And when they got into the boat, the wind ceased (Matthew 14:28-32).

Whenever this passage of Scripture is preached, taught, or spoken about, generally the focus is Peter and Jesus walking on the water. Today, I want to give you a different perspective of the Scripture as given by the Holy Spirit. As we know, Peter and the disciples were on the boat in the middle of the sea, and the waves and winds began to toss the boat. When Jesus went to them, they were afraid because they thought they were seeing a ghost. To confirm the sight was Jesus, Peter asked Him to command him to come to Him. Jesus did so, and Peter exited the boat to walk out to Him. Peter was afraid when he saw the boisterous wind and began to sink. Of course, Peter was saved when he cried out for help, and the wind stopped when they got back into the boat.

You may be saying, "You just summarized the Scripture, so what is the different perspective?" If you step back and look at the situation, the disciples were out at sea on a boat. If you think about a boat and water, there is safety on the boat. When the wind and waves begin to toss the boat, the disciples do not jump off for safety. They stay on the boat. Oftentimes, we stay on our "boat" because we feel it is safe. We feel that we are in a good situation by staying on the boat. But when we think we are in a good situation, something will occur that will send "Greatness" to us.

Oftentimes, we settle on good because we are comfortable with it or feel safe with being good. We allow our comfort to keep us in a good zone instead of stepping out for greatness. When Peter stepped out of the boat, he was going from good to Great! Yes, Jesus came out to the sea, but He didn't initially get in the boat. Peter had to go out to Him first.

We can have greatness in our lives, but we have to go out to get it! We have to focus on greatness to achieve it! Oh, just as the wind distracted Peter as he was walking out to Jesus, we will face distractions when we step out to obtain greatness. But don't let the distraction stop you from achieving greatness! We serve a Savior who will save us when we begin to sink! We serve a Savior who can calm the distractions so we can continue our journey to greatness!

Don't be satisfied with good but desire great! Good things happen within comfort zones, but great things occur when you step out of your comfort zone. In order to be great, you have to step out of good! What you have now is good, but what God has in store for you is great! It's time for you to go from good to great!

MIND YOUR OWN BUSINESS STAY IN YOUR LANE

1 Thessalonians 4:9-12

My fellow brother in the ministry preached a word that revealed something I had never seen prior to the message. The beauty of the revelation was the fact that it was not complex nor did it take an interpreter to interpret the Word. The man of God did not have to exegete the Scripture so the hearers of the Word could comprehend it. It was very clear! I would contend that, oftentimes, we take God's simple Word and make it complicated.

Paul, speaking to the Thessalonians, shared with them one aspect of a life of holiness—brotherly love. We are taught to love one another as God loves us. 1 John 4:7-8 says, "Beloved, let us love one another for love is of God; and everyone who loves is born of God and knows God. He who does not love does not know God, for God is love." Jesus spoke these words in John 13:34, "A new commandment I give to you, that you love one another; as I have loved you, that you also love one another." Brotherly love is not just a thought that applies to the city of Philadelphia, which comes from the Greek words "phila" (love) and "delphia" (brother), but a biblical characteristic that should live and breathe in all of us. Sadly, brotherly love is not exemplified in its fullness today.

We are all guilty of not showing love for our fellow brother or sister. We are *all* guilty at some point in our lives of meddling in the affairs of our fellow brothers and sisters. Instead of being concerned with the dirt in our own houses, we would rather focus on the dirt in front of our brother's front door. We can't aspire to lead a quiet life (peaceful and productive) as Paul stated because we are too busy trying to tell others how to live their lives or being caught up in their matters.

Mind your own business! I was in awe when I read those words. Can you imagine how the world would be if everyone would mind their own business? When you mind your own business, you are more productive! When you mind your own business, you can keep *your* business in order! When you mind your own business, you don't and won't have time to be in business belonging to others (let that marinate).

We could go on and on about this topic. The bottom line is we should show more brotherly love by minding our own business. We should show more brotherly love by staying in our lane! No longer consider it a request from the one whose business and lane you have invaded but see it as a Godly command—mind your own business and stay in your lane!

ALWAYS INTERCEDE FOR OTHERS

1 Timothy 2:1-4

It's amazing how prayer only existed out of convenience. When things were going right, I may have said a prayer once or twice a week. But when all hell was breaking loose, I was praying every day until it stopped. With my lack of understanding in the true power of prayer, I used to think something was wrong with my grandmother when I would walk near her room and hear her praying anytime during the day or before she went to bed at night. It wasn't until I started growing in the Word that I understood the power of not just praying but interceding on behalf of others. It was also mentioned how our prayers are selfish as the words are centered on us. We should pray for ourselves and pray for others, too. "Others" is not exclusive. Prayer should be all-inclusive!

It is imperative that we not only pray for ourselves but intercede for others! We don't know what is going on in a person's life, and to be honest with you, it's really none of our business (yep, I said it). We should be concerned with lifting our brothers and sisters up in prayer and not concerned with what may be tearing them down. We should focus more on praying for our brothers and sisters to come out of what they are in versus thinking about what got them in their current positions.

Again, it's none of our business! Our business is to intercede on their behalf! When Moses was too weak to hold up the rod of God, Aaron and Hur were by his side and helped him raise his arms which led to Joshua and the men's victory over the Amalekites (read Exodus 17:8-16). Moses had help! When we intercede for others, we are their help in their battle!

Let me remind you that you didn't make it this far on your own! God heard the cries of those who interceded on your behalf and look at you now. Enough said!

Please join me in prayer:

"Lord, right now, we come before You to pray not only for ourselves but all of Your children, the believers and the non-believers! We pray for those who are going through a great storm and need You to hold onto in order to get through! We pray for those in need of healing! We pray for those who may be struggling with addiction, depression, or any other mental illness! We pray for those who have lost their peace, their joy, the smile that brightens the day of others! We pray for those who feel like they are constantly spinning their wheels but not making any progress! We pray for those who don't have the faith nor strength to pray for themselves!

"We pray an increased measure of Your Power, Your Protection, Your Presence, Your Grace, Your Mercy, and Your Glory in our lives! Lord, we trust and know You know all and see all so we say this prayer in confidence with faith knowing that You are in control and will take care of Your children! We seal this prayer in the name of Jesus. Amen!"

Always intercede for others!!

Related Reading

Philippians 4:6; James 5:16

PRAYING FOR YOU

Philippians 4:6-7

During a morning commute, the Holy Spirit said, "Pray but not for yourself; pray for others." Oftentimes, we get so caught up in our own storms that we tend to forget about others who are enduring a storm that is either on the same or greater scale than ours. The Holy Spirit spoke these words to me, "Despite the pain you are feeling, pray for others. I will come through for you."

Here is my prayer for you:

"Oh, Heavenly Father, I come before You at this time with a heart of

thanks! Thank You for this day that You have made. I will rejoice and be glad in it! Thank You for allowing me to see another day which is confirmation that Your will for my life is not complete! Father God, I come to You not for me but to intercede on behalf of my brothers and sisters! I don't know what they may be going through right now, but I know You know so I'm asking You to hear their hearts as they cry out to You! Lord, I pray that You renew their strength as they have grown weary and ready to give up! I pray that You give them comfort that will ease their pain! I pray that You will give them the courage to cast their cares upon You so You can have Your way in their storm!

"If they need deliverance, I pray You deliver! If they need a breakthrough, I pray breakthrough is given! If they need peace, I pray You give them a peace that surpasses their understanding! If they need protection, I pray You send an army of angels to encamp all around them and protect them! Lord, I pray that You hear the hearts of Your children and give them what they need in their time of need!

"Prayer changes things, and I know You can make change happen! The effective, fervent prayer of a righteous man avails much. Lord, I may not be the most righteous of Your children, but I have a heart after You and believe my prayer for others will be heard and received! Lord, when You answer the prayers of my brothers and sisters, I pray that they turn around and intercede on behalf of others just as I am doing for them! This is my prayer, and I consider it done in the name of Jesus who said to ask anything in His name because it will be done! Amen!"

My brothers and sisters, hold your head up! Be encouraged! Keep pushing through your pain! Keep pushing through your storm! Don't give up! You got this! Even when you can't pray for yourself, remember someone is praying for you!

Related Reading

2 Chronicles 7:14; Job 42:10; John 14:13-14; 1 Corinthians 10:24; Philippians 2:3-4; James 5:16; 1 Thessalonians 5:11

CONCLUSION: MY POP'S PERSPECTIVE

In writing these last words, I thought long and hard about what to say in this section. Many iterations of this have come and gone due to an inability to settle on one coherent thought or message. So I sat back for a while, and when I say a while, I mean five weeks. But every day at the same time, I would sit and revisit this very same spot. Nothing came to me. Then I realized something that I had overlooked in the purpose of this book. Some will see it as a means to stay spiritually connected or a way to re-focus their spiritual energies. I say it is both and more!

Someone Prayed for Me

When you read this book, I hope you took the time to ponder the words, the anecdotes, and the contextual application of each. There is purpose in it all, but above all else, it is directing you in prayer. Yes, I know prayer is an overused spiritual action with even less meaning because we often are praying all wrong. But hear me now as I give you a small dose of what prayer is and how prayer will matter in the lives of your loved ones and you.

Many moons ago, I visited my paternal grandmother in Birmingham, Alabama. Now I never knew until much later in life why my father had to leave all he knew and loved in Birmingham (1963), a story for another time. But he did, and this was my first time seeing my grandmother and my father's siblings (5). The visit was going great until it came time to go to bed, and my younger uncle Reggie began to pray. I thought it odd, not because he was praying but because I did not know how. Both of my parents were raised in Baptist traditions, yet their first-born, at age nine, did not know how to pray.

My Grandma Kate was mad at my parents, but she quickly got over that since they had already flown back to NYC. Grandma wrote the Lord's Prayer down for me, and I had to recite it twice a day to her and then in front of her before going to bed. Within a week, I knew it, but they were just words until, one night, I was awoken by a terrible thundershower.

All the other kids were asleep, but I could hear someone speaking. I walked through the halls and down the stairs into the parlor. There I found my grandmother kneeling before a portrait of Christ, you know, the one with Christ kneeling at the rock? That portrait is in every house in the south that I know of, but anyway, I stood there listening to her thank the Lord for all that He had done and continued to do in her life, and at the very end, she asked if God could shelter her husband in this terrible storm. It never occurred to me that my grandfather Joe was not home yet. He worked two jobs and long hours on both. That is when I got on my knees, too.

I did not know why I was praying other than I wanted my grandpa home safe. Minutes passed, and my grandmother was still there. She did not stop praying until Grandpa walked through the door. All I remember from the rest of that night was that it was Grandpa who carried me back to bed. This was my first lesson: pray until your prayers are answered.

The next lesson I received came from my grandmother's sister, Bessie. Aunt Bessie was a real entrepreneur in New York City. She took my father in when he first arrived, and he was forever indebted to her until the day she died.

Well, I was always around Aunt Bessie for one thing or another, doing chores, or just sitting in her basement looking at all of the aquariums my uncle Roberto had. I grew up living above them, and she saw all of the trials and tribulations our family went through. Graduating from high school and then joining the Air Force, I made sure to send her a postcard to let her know I was ok. Then, as the many years passed by, through marriages, divorces, and the changes we go through, I found myself sitting at Aunt Bessie's kitchen table. She was much older but still possessed her wit and this uncanny ability to know what you were going through with just one look.

Bessie Alvarez could read a person up and down, which is probably another reason why she was so shrewd in business. However, on this afternoon, my great aunt was recovering from a recent stroke. This was her second one in two years, and it pretty much limited her mobility requiring her to take on a full-time nurse. There we sat face to face for the first time in almost five years. She only had the use of her left arm, and her speech was slower, but you could make out what she was saying. There in the midst of my own personal grief, I sat opposite a woman whom I admired to no end. Then she told me something that has resonated in my being forever.

"JJ, I want you to know something…"

"Yes ma'am," I said easing closer to her.

"I prayed for you…" four simple words that to this day give me pause. I cried then as I do now. To think that someone was praying for me. Through all of my life's difficulties, there was someone praying for my salvation. She knew my pain and that I was suffering. No matter how strong I was on the outside, my aunty *knew* I needed prayers. Those words meant the world to a man, still a little boy, who never knew the love and power of prayer until she opened my eyes that day.

"I prayed for you because I believed in you. You're one good man, and you have made me so proud that my prayers were answered in every way." I held her hand and kissed her cheek as a tear fell. Her nurse came to give her medication, and as I walked outside, the power of her words hit me like a ton of bricks. Bessie Rae Alvarez would succumb to her ailments 18 months later. Another lesson learned: pray for those you love, especially those that have no idea that they need it.

A little more than a year after her death, I found myself deep in despair. It was a horrible place to be. Dark and lonely was the pit. One afternoon, I decided that the pain, doubt, and loneliness were unbearable. Depression's grip tightened like a vice, and I did not know how to get out of it. That is when I remembered my lessons. Each of the teachers had a place, a part of the house where they could connect to their Lord and Savior.

For Kate, it was her parlor, and for her sister, Bessie, it was her kitchen table. Each gave them energy, a spiritual focus. I did not have one in this two-bedroom apartment. So I just prostrated myself across my den, and I prayed the entire night until the dark demons released my spirit at sunrise.

What did I pray for? I prayed for my children and my brother, that Jesus would look over them and all that they do. I prayed so hard for them and took no hope for myself. In this life, that is what I truly love. My children and brother are all I have, and the love I have for them is everlasting. That love, hope, and devotion are what saved me. His plan for me was that I continue loving and being a part of their lives, and to help me do this, He provided me with a house and nice job. Yet there is a place in this house where the positive energies and spiritual healing flows. All who enter sense it without me saying a word. They feel at home and comforted. I devote an hour of each day in this special place, meditating as the sun rises, because that is when I know He is most with me.

As you read these meditations, I hope you found yourself a quiet place where you could feel the presence of good energy. This is your spiritual zone. Sitting there, reading these words, knowing that the most powerful thing you can ever do for someone you love is to pray for them more than you pray for yourself. Trust when I say, "Someone prayed for me," and that has made all the difference in my life.

-James L. Nathan III

Made in the USA
Middletown, DE
23 June 2019